Sam T. Clover

Paul Travers' adventures

Being a faithful narrative of a boy's journey around the world ..

Sam T. Clover

Paul Travers' adventures
Being a faithful narrative of a boy's journey around the world ..

ISBN/EAN: 9783744740951

Printed in Europe, USA, Canada, Australia, Japan

Cover: Foto ©Andreas Hilbeck / pixelio.de

More available books at **www.hansebooks.com**

PAUL TRAVERS' ADVENTURES

BEING A FAITHFUL NARRATIVE OF A BOY'S JOURNEY AROUND THE WORLD; SHOWING HIS MISHAPS, PRIVATIONS AND OFTTIMES THRILLING EXPERIENCES AND HOW HE WON HIS REPORTER'S STAR

BY
SAM T. CLOVER

Chicago
Way & Williams
1897

CONTENTS

CHAPTER		PAGE
I.	WHAT THE EDITOR PROMISED.	5
II.	IN THE HEART OF THE ROCKIES.	21
III.	DOWN TO HARDPAN.	37
IV.	TRAVELING IN QUEER COMPANY.	54
V.	PAUL FALLS AMONG FRIENDS.	72
VI.	A FORTUNE IN EYE-WATER.	90
VII.	IN THE SOUTHERN PACIFIC.	107
VIII.	ABOARD THE CITY OF SYDNEY.	124
IX.	FOLLOWING THE RED WAGON.	142
X.	CIRCUS LIFE IN NEW ZEALAND.	160
XI.	ON SHIPBOARD AGAIN.	178
XII.	WRECK OF THE KOTURAH.	197
XIII.	IN GOOD SAMARITANS' HANDS.	217
XIV.	UNDER THE SOUTHERN CROSS.	236
XV.	RUSTLING IN THE COLONIES.	255
XVI.	EXPERIENCES IN THE ANTIPODES.	273
XVII.	FAREWELL TO AUSTRALIA.	292
XVIII.	LIFE IN THE "GLORY HOLE."	311
XIX.	ABOARD THE CHIMBORAZO.	330
XX.	HEADED FOR HOME.	350

ILLUSTRATIONS

	PAGE
FRONTISPIECE.	1
"PAUL STOOD STOCK STILL."	30
AT THE SECTION HOUSE.	52
AMUSING THE EMIGRANTS.	86
SELLING EYE-WATER AT THE FAIR.	100
DOWN IN THE LAZARETTE.	140
ESCAPING FROM THE SHIP.	148
CIRCUS LIFE IN NEW ZEALAND.	172
ADRIFT ON A QUEER RAFT.	220
PEDDLING "KAISER TINTE" IN SYDNEY.	266
IN THE AUSTRALIAN GOLD FIELDS.	280
PAUL'S FIGHT IN THE GLORY HOLE.	328

Paul Travers' Adventures.

CHAPTER I.

WHAT THE EDITOR PROMISED.

"WELL, my boy, what can I do for you?"

The speaker was chief editorial writer on one of the leading daily papers in the West. Of medium height, fairly robust frame, piercing black eyes, high forehead, and sallow features, his was perhaps the most familiar figure known to the Chicago newspaper world, where his trenchant pen had long since won for him the recognition that his talents deserved.

He now sat in his cozy den on the fifth floor of the Mercury Building, and with his swivel chair half wheeled from his desk turned toward a lad of sixteen, who, straw hat in hand, had just entered the room in response to the invitation that followed his modest tap on the door.

In the bright-eyed, alert figure of the youth who advanced toward him Mr. Wilder recognized the son of an old college friend, whose unpractical business notions, despite his cultured mind, had ever proved a bar to his financial success in bustling, matter-of-fact Chicago.

During the occasional visits paid to his former college chum, Mr. Wilder had learned to admire the younger Paul Travers, whose modest deportment, bright observations, intelligent questions and fund of wit were qualifications that readily attracted the keen newspaper man, who, perhaps, saw in the lad some trace of his former boyhood self.

The cordial greeting he accorded Paul put the latter at his ease immediately. After inquiring if his parents were well, and receiving an affirmative reply, Mr. Wilder divined the youth had come to see him for some specific purpose, and not for a mere friendly call, so, pointing to a chair, in a pleasant tone he asked: "Well, Paul, what's on your mind? What can I do for you?"

Paul's eyes traced the pattern on the carpet for a moment, and then, meeting the kindly gaze of his father's friend, the lad modestly replied: "It's like this, Mr. Wilder: I finished my studies at the high school last month, and knowing that father can't afford to pay my expenses at college, I am anxious to relieve him of my support at home, for you see the dear old pater, with his slender income, has had a hard struggle to provide for mother and the girls and to keep me at school so long. His department chief in the railroad office has offered me a clerkship, but it isn't at all to my taste; in fact, Mr. Wilder," continued Paul, hesitatingly, "I want to do newspaper work and have come up to see if you can give me any encouragement."

Paul blushed as he finished his speech, realizing that his ambition might appear extravagant to the man of ripened experience whom he addressed. Still, as he inwardly reflected, even Mr. Wilder had to have a beginning, and perhaps he might remember this fact.

The editor pulled thoughtfully at his mustache before replying. Then he said: "I don't know any better crude material in the city, my boy, for a future good newspaper man than yourself. But are you sure you have fully considered what you wish? Remember, a reporter's life is not all roses. The pay is small, the snubs are many, and there is no such thing as riches or fame awaiting even him who does his work thoroughly and conscientiously, as I am sure would be the case with you. Better aim for the president's chair in that railroad company, it will bring you more glory and a fuller purse than the editorial management of the biggest newspaper in Chicago."

Paul smiled, but shook his head. "I know that money is a mighty good thing to have, but I assure you, sir, I wasn't cut out for a rich man; you know it isn't in our blood," he added with a pleasant laugh. "I honestly believe I can fit myself for the newspaper profession and hope to attain a moderate success in its ranks. As for the snubs, I am ready to take my share, but I should think if a fellow behaved himself he might expect decent treatment in return."

"So he might, so he might," returned the editor heartily, "and it's not nearly so bad now as when I was a youngster. Well, I find you are determined to break in on us, so I will do all I can to help you along. Let me see, Paul, how old are you?"

"I shall be seventeen in August, sir."

"Pretty young yet to start in, my son. I hate to see you buckle down in earnest without first having a glimpse of the outside world. After once fairly in harness, it is hard to get away, and one draws to manhood and assumes its responsibilities almost before one realizes what has happened. My advice is to roam around a bit before plunging into the stern realities of life. It would be an experience of even far more value than a college training in the calling you wish to follow."

"I feel that you are right, Mr. Wilder; indeed I have often wished that I could be in the position of those wealthy young Englishmen who are sent abroad to make the grand tour after finishing their studies at home; but of course that sort of a trip is out of the question. I can't even afford the economical tramps afoot, such as Bayard Taylor took; but do you know, Mr. Wilder," continued Paul, in his chatty, confidential way, "I have had serious thoughts at times of starting out to see something of the world, regardless of money or prospects. I actually believe I could leave Chicago with just a few dollars in my pocket and circle clear around the globe if I only had the nerve to make the start. Do you think I could succeed?"

The editor laughed grimly. "I believe if anyone could you could, Paul, but it is a more serious undertaking than I should care to essay at my age. With your activity and pluck, however, I guess you would pull through all right, though I am not advising its attempt, mind. Just think over what I have told you and come back to see me next week. Meantime I'll ask the city editor to bear your application in mind."

Paul had the good sense to see that the interview was at an end, so, picking up his hat, he thanked Mr. Wilder warmly for his interest and with a cheery good afternoon, withdrew.

He was unusually quiet that evening, and when his sisters attempted to rally him he let their banter pass almost unheeded. When his mother kissed him good-night she drew her hand caressingly over her boy's face and tenderly inquired if his head ached, but when Paul fondly returned the kiss and assured his mother that nothing ailed him physically her heart told her that the lad was wrestling with some problem which would undoubtedly be revealed in good season.

"Father, I want to walk down town with you," said Paul next morning at the breakfast table.

"All right, my son; I shall be delighted. Have you concluded to take that clerkship after all?"

"No, sir; but I want to have a talk with you." Then, seeing the looks of curiosity depicted on the faces of his sisters, he laughingly added: "Now, girls, just possess your souls in patience and I'll disclose the dark secret this afternoon."

Both Madge and Edith declared they hadn't the least particle of interest in his mysterious plans, and begged him not to think of revealing them on their account, but Paul smiled good-naturedly, and said he knew they were burning with curiosity. To his mother he whispered as she followed his father to the door, "I'll tell you all about it when I come back."

The elder Paul Travers always walked to his office in fine weather. In the first place it saved car fare, and secondly the two-mile tramp acted as a tonic on the system of the man who sat all day at his desk in the auditor's office of the big railroad company where he was employed. Then, too, the miserable street-car service in the west district where he lived repelled rather than attracted passenger traffic.

Father and son traversed several blocks without either saying a word. Suddenly Paul spoke. "Do you think you could get me a pass to Pueblo?" was his startling query.

"I might if I applied for it, I suppose; but what do you expect to do in Colorado?" asked his perplexed parent.

"I went to the Mercury office yesterday," returned Paul, evading a direct reply, "and had a talk with Mr. Wilder about newspaper work. He thought he could help me, but suggested that I see a little of the world and rub off my rawness before starting in as a reporter. He thinks that a practical experience of this sort will be invaluable to me later on. What do you think, father?"

Mr. Travers hesitated. He was proud of his son's energy and ambition, but the boy was dear to his heart, and the thought of any separation was painful. Yet, knowing his own shortcomings, he realized that a journey of the kind proposed would give the lad practical ideas and a knowledge of the world which would at least save him from the fate that had befallen his father. Then, too, he shrewdly guessed that Paul's imaginative mind would never be satisfied with the dull routine of clerical work; so with a rapid mental survey of these various problems he replied: "I certainly believe travel and observation will improve anyone, but, my boy, suppose you go to Colorado. What are your plans?"

"Frankly, I have no definite ones, father. You know I have a standing invitation from Ernest Horton to visit him at Silverton, to which point I would probably go from Pueblo. I am anxious to see some of the famous silver mines in Colorado, and to tramp over part of the Rockies. It seems to me that one who has lived all his life in a flat prairie country might be inspired by the sight of those mighty peaks out there."

"But fifty dollars won't last you very long, Paul. What will you do when your money is gone? I am sorry to say I can't spare any just now."

"Don't you worry about that, dad," returned Paul affectionately. "When my last cent is spent I may take a notion to turn tramp and keep on walking until I strike salt water. But just rest easy. I'm sure I can take care of myself, and I'll keep you all posted so that you may know I am safe and in the land of the living. Only give me your permission to go and help me win mother's consent. Is it a bargain, father?" And the lad halted on the Adams street viaduct, over which they were then passing, and laid his hand caressingly on the elder man's shoulder. "You know what Mr. Wilder's views are," he continued, by way of a clincher, "and I wouldn't urge it myself if I didn't feel certain it was a good thing."

Five minutes more and they had reached the general offices of the railroad company. As Paul turned to retrace his steps his father called from the stairway: "I'll think it over, my son; I'm half inclined to let you go, but I must consult with your mother."

Mrs. Travers was decidedly averse to the project at first, but after a long discussion that night with her husband, during which he told some forcible truths regarding his own early life and its isolation, the mother yielded and reluctantly gave her consent. When Paul outlined his plans and hinted of a possible extension of his Colorado trip to points far beyond, both his mother and the girls thought he was merely joking, and Edith laughed gayly at the notion of any prolonged travels with so slender a purse as Paul carried. None of them could believe he was really in earnest.

In his way Paul was something of a fatalist, and was willing to be guided to a great extent by circumstances. He was determined to travel, and had planned to do any honest work, however humble or rough, in order to succeed in his object. Hard knocks and buffetings he expected to encounter, but if he could have foreseen some of his later experiences even his enthusiasm might have suffered a collapse.

Two days before the time set for starting out on what Madge facetiously termed her brother's "grand tower," Paul made a farewell call on his father's friend at the Mercury office.

"I have come to say good-bye, Mr. Wilder," he said, advancing to where the newspaper man sat at his desk. "You see, I have taken your advice and intend to knock around a little before joining the Mercury staff."

The editor leaned back in his chair until the springs groaned. "Bless my soul, boy, you surely are not in earnest; I never dreamed your parents would give their consent. Which way do you go, and when do you start?"

"I am going to Colorado first and expect to leave Thursday," answered Paul. "I want to see something of the mountainous country and will put in a month or two at the silver mines; what my route will be after that I have not determined. I only know that I intend to keep my face to the West and hope that I won't have to turn in my tracks until I strike Chicago again."

The newspaper man emitted a long whistle. "Well, come, I like that," he ejaculated; "and what do you expect such a trip will cost you?"

Paul smiled. "Well, not much; I have fifty-three dollars in cash and a pass over the Santa Fé road to Pueblo. But I mean to make it, though, sure as I live," added the lad earnestly, noticing the look of incredulity on Mr. Wilder's face.

"Tell you what I'll do, Paul," said the editor banteringly, "I'll give you six weeks to get back to three meals a day and a clean bed. You'll do well if you stand the pressure that long. Why, boy, you'll starve to death out in that country when your money is exhausted."

This light estimation of his powers nettled Paul, as Mr. Wilder had purposely intended, and his tone was a trifle brusque as he retorted: "Oh, no, sir, I guess not, and I am certain you will not see me back here in less than a year, for I will surely go clear around the world. But that isn't all; I hope to get back with more money than I have now, if possible."

Paul was far from being a boaster, and the quiet, earnest manner in which he said this seemed to carry conviction to the quizzical editor, who immediately exclaimed: "Ah, Paul, forgive my skepticism. I haven't the slightest doubt of your ultimate success, and I promise that a first-class position shall be ready for you on the Mercury staff as a reward for your courage and enterprise, when you return. Meanwhile, if you care to send us in any letters descriptive of your travels we will not only publish them but pay you a good price if they prove interesting.

"Do you know, my boy," he continued, "I really am proud of your spirited resolution, and only wish I were twenty years younger, so that I could offer myself as a traveling companion. But don't forget, Paul, that wherever you go or in what company you are thrown you have a good name to cherish and a mother whose heart would be broken if her boy went wrong. Another thing; don't rush into danger needlessly. One can be brave without being foolhardy. I firmly believe you will turn up here some fine morning safe and sound, with a fund of experiences worth the price of one of those silver mines out in the Rockies. So keep a stiff upper lip, my lad, and try to take things philosophically—the feathers with the turkey."

Then this usually cynical leader-writer, whose pen, people said, was tipped with gall, gave Paul a hearty handshake, wished him Godspeed, and as the door closed on his retreating form, muttered, "It's a fool thing to attempt, I am afraid, but if he comes through all right it will be the making of him." Then he whirled around to his desk, dipped his stub pen in the ink and was soon deep in a scathing editorial on the unblushing boodlers of the city hall.

CHAPTER II.

IN THE HEART OF THE ROCKIES.

THE Santa Fé train was speeding rapidly toward Pueblo, and Paul, with the exuberance and elasticity of youth, was beginning to recover from the terrible attack of homesickness that had haunted him since the day previous.

It had been harder to say good-bye to his parents and sisters than he had anticipated, and but for his brave promise made to Mr. Wilder it is possible that he would have abandoned the trip at the last moment when he saw the grief of his mother and the tears of Madge and Edith. But although there was a big lump in his throat and a heaviness of heart that oppressed him sorely, he managed to go through the ordeal without utterly breaking down, and the promise of liberal letterwriting on both sides was a slight measure of comfort.

To the lad who had never before

been out of Illinois the journey so far had been full of novelty. The crossing of the Father of Waters and later of the mighty Missouri were events not to be soon forgotten, while the ever-changing scenery through which the train passed so engrossed his attention that gradually his spirits brightened and his features resumed their accustomed vivacity.

Perhaps it was his lively interest in the surroundings, together with his cheery countenance, which attracted the attention of a young army lieutenant, who presently opened a conversation that, by the time they reached Pueblo, resulted in establishing quite a bond of friendship between the two.

Mr. Hatfield was in the cavalry branch of the service, and was returning to his post on the Colorado frontier, after a two months' leave of absence. He was greatly interested in Paul's proposed trip, and the gentle breeding of the lad, added to the fact that both had recently severed home ties, warmed his heart toward the youngster.

At Pueblo they stayed over night

at the same hotel, where the officer insisted on settling the bill next morning. As the route of each lay in a similar direction, over the Denver and Rio Grande Railroad, both went south on the same train, the presence of the lieutenant adding greatly to the charm of the ride in that picturesque region.

Paul was fairly overcome by the awful grandeur of the mountains, whose beauties he experienced for the first time, and if he said little it was because he was too full for mere words. But there was an exultant leap at his heart and a thrilling of the pulses, as he absorbed the inspiring scenery, that caused his eyes to dilate and his cheeks to blush with gratified pleasure.

Lieutenant Hatfield had business to transact at Fort Garland that would detain him a day and he invited Paul to be his guest at the post. As the lad was in no hurry to reach Silverton, he gladly availed himself of the chance to see something of soldier life on the frontier.

"But you won't see much activity at this post," remarked the lieutenant.

"It is to be abandoned shortly, and only two companies of 'doughboys' remain. Just wait until we reach my command on the Uncompahgre River, then I'll give you a taste of army life."

However, Paul passed a very enjoyable day, especially in the forenoon, when, in company with two young lieutenants fresh from West Point, he hunted jack-rabbits through the scrub oaks and sage brush in the San Luis valley. It was great sport, and as Paul had the good luck to knock over a big jack, he returned to the post elated with his success.

His friend's business proved to be of a nature not suspected by Paul, who incidentally learned that Mr. Hatfield had lost his heart to the charming daughter of a rich rancher down the valley. This accounted for the late arrival of the lieutenant at the post that night after an all day's absence and for the glum looks he wore as they rode to the station next morning in the ambulance.

Paul rallied his friend on his lugubrious aspect, and his lively sallies finally elicited a hearty laugh from the young officer, who apologized for his dullness. At Anamosa they engaged seats in the stage coach which was to carry them through to Lake City, and at 10 o'clock the conveyance started, Paul and the lieutenant settling themselves for an all-night ride to Wagon Wheel Gap.

At daylight the next morning the two comrades jumped out to stretch their cramped limbs and for an hour trudged alongside the horses that toiled up a steep incline. At the summit the driver halted to breathe his team and, pointing with his whip across the intervening valley, oracularly observed: "Deer yander."

Paul's eyes danced with excitement as he took in the graceful contour of the slender animals that, scenting the strangers, suddenly darted back into the woods. Hearing the sigh of disappointment which escaped him the lieutenant laughingly exclaimed: "Never mind, Paul, I promise you plenty of sport when we get to camp."

It had been settled that before going to Silverton Paul was to leave the coach at Los Pinos and accompany Lieutenant Hatfield to his command, which was camped forty miles north of the agency. There had been trouble with the Utes some months previous, necessitating the presence of troops, and although the excitement had abated the regulars still remained in the field.

At Los Pinos an ambulance from the camp was found awaiting the arrival of the coach, into which Paul and his friend climbed, after eating a hearty dinner at the agency mess. A dusty ride through the reservation behind four spanking mules brought them to the camp just in time for supper, to which meal both did ample justice. Paul's appetite, never particularly poor, had materially improved since his advent into Colorado.

The army officers, from the colonel down, gave the young Chicagoan a warm welcome, and Paul spent a very delightful week in their company. Owing to the absence of the captain on sick leave, Mr. Hatfield, as senior lieutenant, was in command of his troop, and he proved a capital host. He arranged many pleasant excursions for the lad, on one of which Paul shot his first big game, a fine buck. He was even permitted to accompany the lieutenant on a scouting expedition in the neighborhood of White River, where some unruly Utes were reported.

This was quite a notable event to him. He was mounted on the lieutenant's spare horse, sported a pair of borrowed spurs, had a big revolver strapped to his belt and, wearing a pair of gauntlets and a gray slouch hat, rode off with the party in gallant style. They were absent from camp four days, during which time they covered 150 miles and saw lots of game, but no Indians. The second day out one of the sergeants shot a magnificent elk, some steaks off which the lieutenant's "striker" broiled for supper. It proved a toothsome dish and, washed down with clear mountain spring water, made a delicious meal.

It was hard to say good-by to his army friends, and especially to the lieutenant, from whom he parted with many expressions of regret, and with the fervent hope of a future reunion. On the way back to the agency the ambulance halted at Chief Ouray's cabin, where Paul met the old warrior and his squaw, Chipeta, who offered him a bowl of soup, but the previous sight of a string of skinned puppies hanging near the shack caused the lad to decline the proffered hospitality.

The fare from Pueblo to Anamosa, thence by stage route to Los Pinos, had made quite an inroad on Paul's slender purse, so, after resting over night at the agency, he decided to send his valise to Silverton by express and set out afoot for that camp.

His outfit consisted of a blanket strapped to his back, in which were a change of underclothing and a few handkerchiefs. On his person he carried a comb, toothbrush, telescopic tin cup, a pocketknife and a small revolver which Lieutenant Hatfield had pressed upon him as a parting gift. The slouch hat that he had worn on the scouting expedition, a woolen shirt and stout shoes completed his tramp attire.

The alkali dust was nearly a foot thick on the trail, so Paul quickly took to the brush, where the startled sage hens flew up almost in his face as he trudged along. For a time he amused himself by popping at them with his revolver, but as he hit none and cartridges were scarce, he soon desisted.

At mid-day he halted near a mountain spring, nibbled some crackers and cheese in the shade of a huge rock and later bathed his swollen feet in the cool stream. It was a scorching hot afternoon, and often Paul was tempted to throw away his blanket, but the thought of a cold night camp proved a stronger argument than the broiling sun. That evening he found lodging at a rough frontier hotel in Ouray and early next morning struck boldly out over the trail, crossing the San Juan divide without any mishap.

At Mineral Point he camped over night, and from there trudged on to Animas Forks. Between that camp and Silverton he had an awful scare. He was plodding through the dust, mentally wondering what Mr. Wilder would think of his experiences, when forty or fifty feet ahead he spied a big black bear with a cub by her side trotting unconcernedly along in the middle of the trail.

Paul stood stock still; then came a strong impulse to turn and run back. But the next minute, to his delight, bruin and her baby slunk off into the timber and disappeared. Paul took no chances, however, but, making a grand detour, did not strike the trail again until he was a mile beyond the dreaded spot. He ruefully thought of his revolver and realized what a poor protection it offered in case he had been compelled to test its powers.

At Silverton, to his great chagrin, Paul found that Ernest Horton was out prospecting near Bridal Veil Basin, and was not expected back until fall. This was a bitter disappointment to the lad, who had counted on a joyful meeting with his former school chum, to whom he had written announcing his prospective arrival. But at the post-office he found a card from Ernest reading as follows:

CAMP CHICAGO, August 13, 188—.
Dear Paul: Inquire at the Silverton Bank for the location of my claim, and come out as soon as you arrive in town. Sorry I can't be

"PAUL STOOD STOCK STILL."

there to meet you, but will let you get even with me up here. Can give you lots of sport and promise you a jolly visit. As ever, your friend, ERNEST.

From the cashier of the bank Paul obtained the desired information, and after getting permission to leave his valise in the office, so as to save storage charges, he renewed his lonely tramp over the mountain trail. He had no difficulty in finding the camp, although it was nearly dark when, in response to his prolonged "Hello, Horton!" the flap of a wall tent was pushed aside and his friend appeared in the doorway, his figure thrown into strong relief by the glare from a generous camp fire.

"By all that's glorious, it's Paul," shouted Horton. "Say, but I'm glad to see you. Come in and meet the boys. Here, Dave, Ned, Harry, let me introduce my friend from Chicago, Paul Travers," and in a minute Paul's hand was warmly gripped by three sturdy young miners, who cordially welcomed him to their camp.

The two friends spent the evening in exchanging mutual reminiscences of school days, Ernest's companions meantime sewing industriously on certain garments that needed repairing. Occasionally they interrupted the flow of conversation to ask some questions, but only at rare intervals, so that when it was time to turn in each had pumped the other nearly dry.

Ernest warmly approved Paul's design to put a girdle around the globe, but said he had no intention of letting him start until he had paid the camp a long visit. He explained that he and his three comrades had formed a partnership to do prospecting that season and had entered several promising claims, one of which they expected to sell to a Boston syndicate. The fishing in the mountain streams was good, the hunting was excellent, and if Paul wanted other exercise he might handle a pick and shovel on one of their recently acquired "prospects."

Ernest was a royal good fellow, and his partners proved to be a jolly trio, who insisted on treating Paul as a guest and giving him the best of everything, despite his protests. The healthy outdoor existence, good hours and plain food imparted a rich color to the lad's cheeks and sent the blood coursing through his veins, so that when the time for leaving arrived he felt strong enough to surmount any and all obstacles.

It had been a delightful fortnight. Hunting, fishing and exploring mountain fastnesses had caused the days to glide by all too swiftly, so that Paul was reluctant to leave the camp. But he had determined to reach the coast before cold weather should catch him en route, so he manfully resisted the appeals of his friends to remain longer, and one bright, crisp morning toward the 1st of September started down the trail with a hearty Godspeed from the quartet that assembled to see him off.

In his pocket he carried a letter of introduction to the agent of the stage line at Silverton, who was a brother to Dave Enderley, one of Ernest's partners. Guessing the state of Paul's finances, Dave had suggested that he could just as well save him coach fare to Gunnison City, to which point the stage ran. Paul gladly accepted the proffered kindness, for he dreaded the return tramp over the divide, the recollection of his narrow escape from the bear being still fresh in his mind.

The agent proved to be all that Dave had depicted him, and Paul was deadheaded through to Gunnison, the only expense being his meals on the road. But even these were costly, and when he alighted from the coach at Gunnison City his stock of cash was reduced to three dollars. The situation began to grow serious, but Paul knew that sooner or later his purse would be emptied, so he did not borrow trouble.

After registering at the only hotel the place afforded he scrubbed off some of the dust and dirt, ate a dubious meal and then strolled over to what the old-timers called "Newtown," a collection of tents and board shanties that marked the more recently settled portion of Gunnison City.

The main street presented an odd appearance to the eyes of the observant lad. Dance halls, hurdy-gurdy saloons, cheap clothing stores and gambling houses constituted the "substantial" buildings, which consisted of hastily constructed shanties of dressed lumber that were conspicuous because of their contrast with the prevailing style of tent architecture.

There was the usual medley of mixed characters that may be met in all new camps. Clerks from the states in feverish search for riches and with poorer prospects of getting them than ever before; typical miners, stage drivers, bullwhackers, gamblers, loafers and roughs of all descriptions, with here and there a gaudily dressed female—the advance guard of her gentler sisters. No wonder Paul was fascinated by the strange sights; the atmosphere he breathed fairly teemed with excitement.

A crowd that was constantly passing in and out of one of the wooden palaces attracted his attention, and with boyish curiosity he strayed inside with the rest. A dance was in progress on the sanded floor, the bars on either side of the room were doing a flourishing business, while away at the rear end a number of gamblers bent over a green table where a man sat dealing cards from a polished steel box

Just as Paul approached this corner there was an excited protest from one of the players, followed by loud and angry cries of profanity. Next instant was heard a sharp report, and with a fearful groan the disputant fell in a nerveless heap to the floor, his late associates hastily scattering in a dozen different directions.

In the rush Paul was borne swiftly out doors and before he could fully realize what had happened he found himself running a foot race with a strapping young fellow, who led the way in the direction of "Oldtown," and whose long mustache fluttered like the streamers on a masthead, as they breasted the keen night air.

CHAPTER III.

DOWN TO HARDPAN.

Presently both slackened their speed and settled into a walk.

"Pretty tough experience that," observed Paul's companion, with a backward wave of his hand. "Mighty glad to get away with a whole skin, weren't you?"

"I should think so. I had no idea what sort of a den it was or I guess I should have kept out. Nice reception to give a stranger, isn't it?"

The other laughed. "Oh, well, it's what you must expect in these boom towns, where all the scum of civilization is collected; ain't a bit sorry I'm going away."

"Then you don't live here?"

"Oh, no; my home is in Denver; my two partners and I had an offer of plenty of carpenter work at pretty stiff prices; so as trade was dull at home this summer we came up here by wagon; but we are going back to-morrow."

"To Denver?" queried Paul, wistfully.

"Yep! Don't live there, do you?"

"No, but I am headed that way. I suppose there's no chance to join your party, is there?"

"I don't know; can you cook?"

Visions of his experiences in camp at Bridal Veil Basin came to Paul's mind as he hesitatingly answered, "Well, I'm not an expert, but I can make good coffee and can turn a flapjack without spilling the batter in the fire."

"Where are you staying?"

"Over at the Gunnison House."

"Oh, yes; we're camped near there; that's our tent just the other side of the prairie schooner you see with the green box. Tell you what I'll do. I'll speak to the boys to-night about it, and if you're up before we get away in the morning perhaps I can fix you out."

Paul was profuse in his thanks and eagerly promised to be on hand. He did not sleep soundly owing to the number of bedfellows that forced their acquaintance, and he was glad to turn out at daybreak and settle his bill. He had just a dollar left when this was done.

His companion of the previous night was vigorously splashing around in a tin basin as Paul neared the wagon with the green box. Presently he looked up and with a cheery "Hello, stranger, you did make it, didn't you?" motioned him to a seat on an inverted bucket.

"Well, what luck?" was Paul's anxious salutation.

"First rate. We don't really need a cook, but I managed to talk the boys into the idea, so they agreed you might join us. Got any baggage?"

"I have a valise at the hotel."

"Better get it over here, then, because we want to make an early start."

Paul fervently expressed his obligation for these good offices and made a bee-line for the hotel, returning in a few minutes with his grip.

"Had breakfast?" asked his new acquaintance, who introduced himself as Jack White.

"No; I was too early and didn't wait for fear of missing you."

"All right; might just as well pitch in now and show what you can do. There's the coffee beans and you'll find plenty of kindling under the wagon."

By the time the rest of the outfit was up and dressed Paul had a good fire blazing and a pot of coffee almost boiled. With the handle of a hammer inserted in a mustard can he had pounded his beans on the tire of a wagon wheel until they were pretty well pulverized, and having mixed up a batter and heated his pan he was ready to fry the flapjacks. Luckily, everything went off without a hitch and Jack's two comrades voted the new cook a success.

Down the Tomichi River, over Marshall Pass and across the South Park, the little caravan wended its way, averaging from twenty-five to thirty miles a day. A saddle horse that had been bought from an impecunious prospector was allotted to Paul, who generally rode ahead of the party and selected the camp for the night.

The hunting and fishing were prime, his duties were not exacting, and his companions were sociable and good-natured, so that the trip to Denver was almost like a continuous picnic to the young traveler, who was actually sorry when the capital city of the Centennial State was reached.

Paul's first night in Denver was passed on a pile of shavings in the workshop occupied by Jack White and his two friends. It was not a choice couch, but this was no time to be squeamish, and wrapped in his faithful blanket the lad slept as contentedly as if he were in his own bed at home.

"You can hold this down as long as you stay here," said Jack, "but I suppose you will be moving toward the slope before the week's out, eh?"

Paul thought he might, but hadn't quite decided just when he would leave town. He was grateful to Jack for his kind offer, however, and told him so.

"Oh, that's all right. Don't cost a cent and I guess you won't steal anything; you look honest."

A budget of news from home awaited him at the postoffice in answer to his letters mailed at Silverton. All wondered how he could possibly travel around so much on his slim capital, and expressed the hope that he would soon be with them again.

But Paul had no intention of returning yet. He was fairly imbued with the spirit of travel and was determined to prove to Mr. Wilder that it was no idle boast he had made. It did seem to be a foolhardy undertaking, as he mentally confessed that noon, when, after writing the folks to direct their next letters in care of the general delivery at San Francisco, he sat with his last quarter in his pocket, eating dinner in a cheap restaurant on Holliday Street.

Perhaps it was the grim humor of the situation that lent a flavor to the meal which the cooking could never have imparted. After settling his bill he would be down to hardpan, but instead of feeling alarmed he had only curiosity to know how he would fare. He stoutly rejected the suggestion that at times insinuated itself of writing home for funds, for, although he knew they would be forthcoming, he was also aware how illy his father could spare any money.

"No, I must get out of town, and at once," was his final conclusion. "If I have to work for my meals I might just as well do it on the road. I'll start to-day—now—just as soon as I finish my dinner."

Paul had been in Denver about a week. He had sold his valise and reduced his wardrobe to the single change of underclothing strapped in his blanket. His marching attire was the same as when he was tramping over the mountain trails. There was no ticket to buy, no trunk to check, and no farewells to make, except to shake hands with Jack White. All he had to do was to strike the railroad track and follow the ties until he reached the Union Pacific junction near Cheyenne, which meant a tramp of about 140 miles. He figured that he could do this easily in six days.

Paul was a novice at track walking and after covering the first five miles he felt very tired, but he kept doggedly on, as he had planned to pass the night at Golden, fourteen miles from Denver.

While he was limping along feeling decidedly uncomfortable and lonesome he came suddenly to a culvert on which was seated a tall, slim lad perhaps a year older than himself.

"Walkin' good?" the latter asked, quizzically, as Paul stepped on the cross-ties.

"Not particularly. How far is it to Golden?"

"Six miles."

Paul groaned. "Why, a man back there about a mile said it was only three."

"Yes? Well, lem'me tell you that the fellows out here make mighty curious calculations. A Colorado mile's equal to two ordinary ones back East, 'specially if you're walkin'. Goin' to stay long at Golden?"

"Only over night; I'm on my way to Cheyenne."

"Walk?"

"I guess so."

"Well, that's what I call a piece of luck; bound that far myself. What do you say, shall we hoof it together?"

Paul signified his willingness and sitting on the culvert with his feet dangling alongside those of his companion's the two compared notes. Neither had a nickel, but both were headed for San Francisco and they solemnly shook hands to go through as "partners." Paul's new acquaintance said his name was Dick Tracy; that he had wandered up to Colorado from Texas and had concluded to spend the winter in California.

He was a lively youth with a fund of entertaining stories regarding his cowboy adventures in the Lone Star State; not particularly clever, but sharp-witted, owing to his long contact with the world. His experiences gained while on the tramp were invaluable to them in their present plight, as Paul presently discovered.

The miles now seemed much shorter, and it was not long before the smoke from the smelters at Golden were uncovered. The 6 o'clock whistles were just sounding as they passed the little station and their piercing shriek seemed to intensify the fact that it was supper time.

"See here," observed Dick, as the two sat on an empty soap box at the end of the platform, "you're new to this sort o' thing. Wait here for me while I go up town and rustle for supper. I'll be back in three shakes of a lamb's tail, see if I don't," and before Paul could enter a protest he was off.

Dick managed to keep his word, returning in about ten minutes with several slices of bread and butter and some cold steak that he said the cook in an eating house had handed him from the back door. As both were hungry they made short work of the provisions, afterward rinsing their throats at a big tank near the station.

"Looks dubious, doesn't it?" remarked Paul as they sat on the edge of the platform an hour later after having searched in vain for an empty car in which to pass the night.

"That's what!" returned Dick, sententiously. "Guess we'll have to crawl under that pile o' ties stacked over yonder; it's the best thing in sight."

It was a chilly retreat, but the boys

were pretty tired and slept soundly with Paul's blanket wrapped around their shoulders. They awoke early, made their toilet at the tank, and at 6 o'clock Dick said he guessed he'd go up and strike the cook for breakfast.

He was absent about half an hour, but returned with full hands. "Had to split some wood," he explained. "Cook said he wouldn't feed no more tramps unless they did a spell o' work. Didn't hurt myself, though," he added, with a chuckle. "Pitch into this stuff, Paul; I ate all I could hold up there."

From Golden to Boulder, thence to Longmont, Loveland and Fort Collins, the two lads tramped, sleeping in empty box cars or in deserted section-houses, as the opportunity presented. Paul had managed to overcome his repugnance to ask for food, but never failed to offer his services first. Sometimes he was given a stick or two of wood to saw, but more often than not his fresh young face won the desired meal without further parleying.

The worst part of the journey was

now before the pair. From Fort Collins to Lone Tree stretched a thirty-mile desert, absolutely without shade or water; so, after a long discussion, the lads decided to wait until sunset before attempting its passage. They passed the afternoon in sleeping near the fair grounds, and on awaking had a refreshing bath in an irrigating ditch adjacent. Toward 6 o'clock the boys made a sorry meal on the remnants saved from dinner, after which they bravely started down the track on their all-night tramp.

The first few hours were beguiled by lengthy dissertations on favorite delicacies, in which each minutely described his ideal dish, but finding this was provocative of hunger, they finally desisted and settled into a dogged walk. Toward midnight the wind came on very fresh, and the howling of the coyotes on both sides of the track rendered the lads slightly uncomfortable, but they kept closely together, and although neither could see the other, they gathered courage from their companionship.

It was a long night and a tedious

tramp, so that the first gray streaks of dawn seemed vexatiously slow in appearing. Sunrise found them in the vicinity of a deserted section-house two miles from Lone Tree, with a record of twenty-eight miles to their credit. Utterly exhausted, the boys spread out their single blanket, and, throwing themselves upon it, sank immediately into deep slumber.

The sun was high in the heavens when Paul awoke, hungry and stiff after his long walk. Dick was still snoring in the shade of the shanty, where he had unconsciously rolled to escape the downpouring rays of the sun. A shout from his comrade caused him to open his eyes, emit a long yawn, and to wonder how long they had slept.

"Must be nearly noon, I should judge," said Paul, glancing upward. "Time we were moving on to Lone Tree to capture breakfast."

Lone Tree consisted of a single ranch and the new section-house. Dick said he would take the ranch while Paul went on to try his luck at the red-painted house adjoining the track.

4

A little woman, carrying a big baby, answered his knock at the kitchen door.

"Can you do anything to pay for a dinner?" she said, repeating Paul's question, meantime eyeing him critically. "I guess you can. Jest take that bucket and go to the tank and fill it with water; after that mebbe I'll have somethin' for you to eat."

Paul trudged off with the wooden pail, and, presently returning, set it down in the kitchen sink. A big pile of unwashed dishes stood on a low bench, and through an open doorway the remnants of a meal were discernible on the dining-room table.

While Paul discussed a generous plate of corned beef and cabbage the little woman sat on a chair and told her troubles. She was the wife of the section boss, with six men to board; her baby was only a month old and her hired girl had left her only two days before on half an hour's notice. She was utterly tired out and would feel very grateful if Paul would stay and assist her in the kitchen until she could engage help from Cheyenne.

As the delay of a few days mattered little to Paul he readily consented to remain and cheerfully set to work on the pile of dishes as soon as he finished his dinner, or, rather, breakfast. When Dick came up an hour later he found Paul installed at an open window in the little sitting-room with a fat baby in his lap that was crooning away in great glee.

"Must ha' struck some o' yer relations, I reckon," ejaculated Dick, with a broad grin on his freckled face.

"No, sir; I have hired out as assistant dishwasher and nurse to the family. Please go away; we don't want any tramps around here." Then, as Dick grinned again in appreciation of this joke, Paul asked, "Did they treat you well over yonder?"

"Jest a hand-out, that's all. No good there to-night, though," added Dick, disconsolately.

"Oh, well, I guess I can fix you out if you hang around here, but keep shady, as I wouldn't want them to think I was in league with a gang of tramps."

Paul stayed three days at the section-house, at the end of which time the little woman had inveigled a stout Norwegian girl from Cheyenne to Lone Tree. The section boss gave him two dollars for his trouble and passed him on to Union Pacific junction by the regular passenger train. Dick had gone up the night previous on a freight, having agreed to meet Paul at the junction next day.

And there they did meet, but not as either had expected. When Paul jumped from the train he asked one of the station hands if he had seen a lad answering to Dick's description.

"Sort of a tall, freckled-faced duck, with long hair an' high cheek bones, wan't he?"

"Yes, I guess that's Dick."

"Well, I reckon he's in the freight-house stretched out acrosst two barrels, deader'n a door nail; the crowner's in there now."

"Dead! Dick dead! What do you mean?"

"Killed last night on No. 6. Went ter sleep on the brakes an' got his head crushed. You'll find out all ther

AT THE
SECTION HOUSE.

perticklers in there if you ask ther crowner."

It was horrible, but only too true, as Paul discovered when he entered the freight room. His late comrade lay outstretched on a board, around which stood six men in charge of the coroner from Cheyenne, a verdict of accidental death while stealing a ride having just been rendered.

There was nothing on the body to identify the remains, and Paul could only say that the name of the dead lad was Tracy and that his home was somewhere in Texas. As this information shed no light on the case the coroner curtly ordered the body to be sent to Cheyenne for burial, and the last look Paul had of his late companion was when he lay in a cheap pine coffin awaiting transportation to the city. He turned away with a sickening feeling at his heart. It might be his fate any moment.

CHAPTER IV.

TRAVELING IN QUEER COMPANY.

For many hours Paul wandered aimlessly through the streets of Cheyenne, so utterly depressed in spirit because of Dick's tragic death that he felt no desire to eat, even had he possessed the means to pay for a meal. About 4 o'clock in the afternoon, when his stomach vigorously rebelled against its prolonged fast, the lad mechanically bent his steps toward a restaurant, but just before entering it he suddenly remembered that the money given him by the section boss was gone.

On the way to Cheyenne from the junction Paul had encountered a gang of tramps, some of the members of which had relieved him of his blanket and underclothes and coolly appropriated his knife, revolver, tin cup and the two-dollar bill, but had allowed him to retain his tooth brush and pocket comb, for which articles, apparently, none of the party had the slighest use.

Thankful to get off with a whole skin, and with the clothes he wore, Paul had submitted philosophically to the robbery, seeing that it was worse than useless to enter any protest, but the incident had not tended to elevate his spirits, and, more downhearted than ever, he continued his tramp into town. Turning disconsolately from the restaurant he spied a pleasant-faced boy standing in the doorway of a grocery store, with whom, after a short parley, he managed to trade a natural agate for a piece of cheese and a handful of crackers.

The edge of his hunger worn off, he continued his tramp around town until the gathering dusk warned him he had better hunt sleeping quarters for the night. At 9 o'clock, after meeting repeated rebuffs, Paul grew desperate, and approaching a blue-coated man standing under a gas lamp inquired if he could help him to a night's lodging.

"Can I? Well, I should say so. What are you doing around here, anyway?" the man demanded in an authoritative voice.

Paul explained that he was a stranger and had no money.

"Oh, you haven't, eh? Well, I can fix you out, young fellow; just come with me," and up the street he started, half dragging the unwilling lad, who began to suspect the lodging provided might not be at all to his liking.

This suspicion shortly became a certainty, when, after traversing a few blocks, the burly stranger pushed the hesitating youth up a stairway, over the entrance to which was a lamp bearing the legend "City Hall" in black letters on the glass. Down a long corridor Paul was marched by his captor, who by this time had announced himself as the city marshal.

Halting before an iron-grated door the officer produced a big key, which he fitted to the lock and turned the bolt back with a smart snap that sent a shiver through the frame of his prisoner, who realized with painful suddenness that he was about to be thrust into jail. The thought was so agonizing that he turned fiercely upon the marshal and protested vehemently against the indignity.

"You keep quiet, youngster, or mebbe you'll get more than you bargained for. We have just one place for all tramps and vagrants. Inside here you stay until 8 o'clock to-morrow morning, and if you don't pull your freight then, lively, like as not you'll get sent up for sixty days."

It was a bitter dose for the poor lad, but Paul had no recourse. Argument with the bullet-headed officer was useless, so, swallowing his indignation along with a few salty tears, he passed through the heavily barred door, which closed with a bang. Then Paul found himself in a large cell, in the center of which a smoky oil lamp shed its dim rays over the room, emitting at the same time a most villainous smell.

As soon as he became accustomed to the uncertain light Paul discerned a dozen shapeless forms, wrapped in blankets, strung out around the brick-walled chamber, from some of which the most unmelodious snores emanated. A drunken brute in one corner, who persisted in filling the air with his idiotic yells, was being kicked into silence by two wakeful tramps, whose rest the noisy reveler had disturbed, and a general uprising was threatened, when the crazed wretch fell back into unconsciousness and the agitated blankets returned to their former appearance of torpidity.

Not a pleasant situation for a delicately nurtured lad to be placed in, and Paul's heart was like lead as he thought of passing the night in such hideous company. A single window at the farther end of the cell, guarded by iron bars, admitted a sickly glare from a street lamp, and toward this spot Paul picked his way, the broad sill suggesting to him, in the absence of chair or table, a possible camping place for the night where he would at least be semi-detached from the other inmates.

With his back against the casing and his feet planted on the opposite side, Paul managed to snatch a few hours of sleep, but racking nightmares haunted his rest and several times before daylight he awoke from frightful dreams, in which he suffered mental tortures.

The first to open his eyes in the morning, he had ample opportunity to study his fellow lodgers before they awoke. A more disreputable gathering it would have been hard to find anywhere, and Paul shuddered as he surveyed the brutal faces of the sleepers, who appeared even more repulsive in the gray dawn.

On the walls of the cell, once white, were scratched dozens of fanciful, if not elegant, nicknames of the various choice visitors that on former occasions had been compulsory guests of this queer lodging house. Here and there were grinning skulls, startlingly suggestive hanging scenes, hideous caricatures, ribald verses, and other illustrations of like nature, penciled by rude artists whose term of incarceration had been beguiled in this manner. The lad's cheeks burned with honest blushes as he contemplated this offensive decoration, and he suddenly experienced an acute nostalgic attack that almost made him forswear his tramp and resolve to return home.

Suddenly he was aware of a pair of black eyes watching him from below, and presently their owner straightened up, threw off his blanket, and disclosed the features of a man who might have been anywhere between the age of thirty and forty, a closer estimate being impossible to make, owing to the accumulation of dirt he carried.

"Whatcher in fer?" he demanded of Paul. "Liftin'?"

Paul was shrewd enough to guess this meant stealing, so he shook his head negatively, adding, half humorously: "Reckon the marshal was afraid I might run away with the town, though, so he put me in here for fear of accidents."

The owner of the black eyes and dirty face condescended to grin at this flippancy and then observed, "Trampin' it, eh?"

"Trying to," answered Paul. "I want to get through to San Francisco."

"'Frisco? Oh, yer do! Goin' ter walk there, I s'pose? Nice time ye'll have crossin' the mountains. Me an' Seldom Seen's bound that far, but we don't do no walkin', though, does we, Seldom?" and the speaker turned toward a man with a grizzled beard whose frowzy head had just emerged from a villainous blanket.

"Not none," growled the newly-awakened tramp. "We never walks nowheres, we don't."

"But you can't afford to ride all the time, though, can you?" queried Paul.

The grizzled tramp laughed derisively at this exhibition of innocence.

"O' course we kin. An' we allers takes a Poolmin box-car an' has ther drorin'-room section ter ourselves." Then, with mock gravity, he inquired of his partner: "Jimmy, did yer engage er t'rough sleeper to Ogden fer us las' night?"

"Ye bet I did," answered his comrade, whose full cognomen Paul discovered was Jimmy-Hit-the-Road-a-Welt. "Got a private parler reserved, an' we pulls out ter night, sure."

"Good 'nuff," returned Seldom

Seen. "That'll get us ter Salt Lake nex' Friday."

In his talks with Dick Tracy Paul had learned how cleverly the expert tramps "spring" open the doors of box-cars to steal rides; but he also knew that it was a dangerous practice as well as a state's prison offense; yet he was strongly tempted to ask these two worthies to let him accompany them, if only for the sake of the experience he might gain. He determined to make the venture.

"Say, Jimmy," he began, somewhat nervously, "do you suppose I could join you and Seldom Seen in this trip, or will it interfere with your plans?"

"Come, fer all I keer," said Jimmy. "Wot do you say, Seldom?"

"I sez let ther kid in ef he ain't afraid ter resk his precious carkiss."

"It's a go, then," cried Paul, by way of a clincher, "and I'm willing to take all chances if you are."

By this time the rest of the inmates of the cell had come out of their semi-comatose state, and presently a jailer appeared with some chunks of coarse, dry bread and a big pannikin full of steaming liquor which Jimmy declared was "corfy." Paul scalded his mouth with a cup of the dark mixture and gnawed away at the dry bread, a thick slice of which was tossed to him by the surly official, whose curses were liberally bestowed with his more tangible offerings.

Half an hour later the door opened again and the city marshal entered to release those against whom no charges were pending. Paul was dismissed with a caution; while Seldom Seen and Jimmy-Hit-the-Road-a-Welt were threatened with severe penalties if they did not make themselves scarce. Then the chief of police pointed to the door, and Paul, followed by Seldom Seen and Jimmy, led the way downstairs and out into God's fresh air, which to the lad had never before seemed so pure and precious.

"Ain't got any scads, I persume?" was Jimmy's first question, when the trio had put several blocks between them and their late sleeping quarters.

"I suppose you mean money," returned Paul. "I had two dollars yesterday, but I fell among thieves on my way to Jericho—I mean Cheyenne—and they 'lifted,' as you call it, all my loose change, together with various other of my belongings. No, I am sorry to say I am flat broke."

"Oh, well, it ain't no consekence," said Jimmy, grandiloquently. "Seldom Seen kin step inter ther First Nash'nal Bank an' get a draft cashed, can't yer, old man?"

"Onforch'nitly ther ain't nobody here as kin identerfy me, 'cept ther city marshal," remarked Seldom, with a serious air, "an' I hates ter ask any favors from these yer petty offishals. Reckon we'll have ter worry along ontel I gets my nex' remittance at Salt Lake."

"You see, we'll have ter take along some grub," explained Jimmy, "but, in course, if you're broke yer can't do nothin'. Me and Seldom'll put in ther day rustlin' an' mebbe you'd better try yer luck, too, 'cause we'll need three or four days' rations, sure."

"Tell you what I'll do," exclaimed Paul, a brilliant idea occurring to him.

"I'll go out to Camp Carlin, where I have some army acquaintances, and I shouldn't wonder if they'll let me have enough provender for us all. What do you think of the scheme?"

The two professionals both heartily approved it, and after designating a rendezvous for that evening, this curiously assorted trio separated, Paul starting out on a brisk walk for Camp Carlin, which lay three miles north of the city.

Lieutenant Hatfield had often spoken to Paul of a classmate named Boyd, who was stationed at Carlin, and whom he had painted as a royal good fellow. It was on the bare chance of finding him at the post that Paul based his hopes of success. Fortunately he was not doomed to disappointment, and Paul had only to introduce himself as a friend of Hatfield's to be cordially welcomed and entertained by the lieutenant, who later loaded him down with provisions from his own mess when he learned of its contemplated use.

In the basket, which the lieutenant's "striker" had filled with cold chicken, fresh bread and several pies, was also placed a small flask of brandy that Mr. Boyd suggested would be useful in case any of the party should fall ill on the journey. Thus liberally weighted down Paul set out at dusk for the city, heading direct for the rendezvous, where he found his queer acquaintances awaiting his arrival.

As soon as it was fairly dark the three started for the railroad yards, accompanied by a friend of Jimmy's, who had been impressed to cover up their tracks, after breaking into the car. Seldom Seen led the way straight toward some freight cars standing on a side-track that were awaiting transportation to the West, and which he had previously located. With a beating heart, Paul watched, while the three experts, with incredible swiftness, unscrewed the nuts that held fast the sliding door of the box-car, and then, by means of a flat board used as a lever, pried the door open from the bottom until there was space enough to admit a human being. This done, Seldom Seen quietly and dexterously wriggled into the car, motioning Paul to follow. Awkwardly enough, and with some trepidation, the lad shinned through the aperture, but not without severely bruising his shoulder-blades and knees in the attempt.

Jimmy next passed up the basket of provisions and two lard cans filled with water, which Seldom Seen carefully stowed away in a secure place. Then, as silently and as skillfully as his partner, Jimmy wormed himself through the opening and called softly that everything was all right. The next minute the board was withdrawn, the door sprung back into position, the nuts carefully replaced by the friendly tramp, and Paul was left in inky darkness with two presumably tough citizens whom he had known just eighteen hours. No wonder that he was seized with a sudden nervous fit and an ardent desire to be safe outside breathing the free air of Heaven again.

Barely had the trio managed to fit into comfortable niches among the merchandise piled in the car when a noise outside proclaimed the appearance of the yardmen for the purpose of making up a train. Backward and forward from one track to another the car was switched until the entire train, composed of fast freight, was ready for its journey to the West. Meantime absolute silence was maintained by the imprisoned tramps, for the yardmen have quick ears, and discovery meant at least sixty days in the county jail. By the time the train was ready to start Paul's uneasiness had subsided to such an extent that he dozed off into unconsciousness, from which he did not emerge until the night had far advanced and the incessant rumbling of the wheels and continuous jerking of the cars told him he was fairly started on his journey toward the Pacific Coast.

The atmosphere in the car was heavy and almost stifling, a small grated aperture near the roof at one end admitting homeopathic doses of fresh air. A violent headache that soon attacked Paul rendered sleep out of the question, and as he tossed restlessly on the hard boxes that formed his couch his thoughts were not of the pleasantest. Visions of dreadful accidents floated before his perturbed brain, and all the newspaper reports that he had read of railroad disasters were painfully fresh in his memory. When at length he did sleep it was only to experience a series of dire mishaps in his troubled dreams, which were so realistic that he awoke from time to time with the perspiration standing in big beads on his forehead.

He heard his companions conversing in low tones when he finally regained consciousness next morning, but his head was so hot and his throat so dry that his voice sounded like its own ghost when he asked softly for a drink of water. A pull at the tin pail helped to freshen him up a bit, and a dash of brandy that Jimmy insisted on his swallowing cured the sickness in his stomach caused by the motion of the car. Conversation all that day and the next was confined to whispers, the constant passing and repassing of the brakemen overhead rendering such a precaution necessary. All three ate and drank sparingly, most of the time being spent in sleeping. Two days and two nights of this was an experience that Paul mentally determined should never be repeated, but he wisely refrained from giving voice to his thoughts and outwardly appeared perfectly reconciled to the situation.

Several long halts had been made at intervals during the trip, but the two old-timers knew the route so well that they made no movement to get away, and it was not until the car was finally detached from the train and side-tracked that Jimmy announced their arrival at Ogden. It was the morning of the third day, and knowing that the car contained perishable merchandise, the trio hoped for speedy release from their prison. Nor were they disappointed. Soon after daylight voices were heard outside, the seal of the car was broken, and presently the door was rolled back, admitting a flood of delicious fresh air to the three tramps, who, concealed behind some boxes, awaited an opportunity to jump and run.

"Now's our chance," whispered Jimmy, after taking a hurried survey of the field. The yardmaster had disappeared and the teamster was busy with his horses. "All together, now, jump!" In spite of their cramped limbs the three managed to make a fairly creditable leap, and away across the tracks they dashed, into the shadow of a convenient lumber pile, almost before the astonished driver knew what had happened.

There was no pursuit, as they quickly discovered, to Paul's infinite relief, and after ten minutes' rapid walking all three stopped to take a breather, which was rendered imperative by their long inactivity.

CHAPTER V.

PAUL FALLS AMONG FRIENDS.

"Oh, but I'm glad to get out of that prison," Paul feelingly remarked as soon as he had recovered his wind.

"Lots o' wuss places 'n that," said Jimmy, sententiously.

"Well, I hope I'll never find them," was the fervent rejoinder. "But, say, fellows, what are your plans?"

"Me and Jimmy's goin' ter let Ogden take keer of us fer er few days," broke in Seldom Seen; "an' mebbe longer, if the city marshal ain't too pertickler 'bout our health. You said you was goin' ter Salt Lake, didn't yer?"

"Yes," returned Paul in a decided tone, glad in his heart to know that he could part company with this queer pair without appearing ungrateful. "You see, I'm anxious to take a peep at the tabernacle and other of Brigham Young's curios, to say nothing of a plunge in the big salt lake. Better come along."

"Not none," growled Jimmy. "Had all we wanted o' Salt Lake last time we went up, eh, Seldom?"

"I should smile," observed that worthy, scratching his grizzled chin. "Some o' them Mormons is wuss'n a reg'mint o' depperty sher'ffs. Ain't got no regard for travelin' toorists, they ain't."

Paul laughed merrily. "Oh, that's the way the wind blows, is it? Well, then, I won't urge you. Just put me on the right road and I'll pull out lively."

"Easy done, that," drawled Seldom Seen, gathering his loose limbs together and slowly rising. "All ye hev ter do is ter folly ther track off there ter the left an' keep walkin' till yer gits ter ther city."

"How far do you call it from Ogden?"

"'Bout thirty miles or so, I reckon."

Paul groaned. "Nice prospect for a fellow with tender feet. Well, there's no help for it, I guess, so the sooner I start the better."

The lad put out his hand, and, awkwardly enough, wrung the grimy paw of Seldom Seen, then performed the same operation on Jimmy-Hit-the-Road-a-Welt, both worthies stoically enduring the novel experience without uttering a word.

The two stood watching the youngster until his lithe figure had almost disappeared from view, each with a queer expression on his countenance.

It was Jimmy who spoke first. "Well, I'm blowed," was his earnest if somewhat inelegant ejaculation. "He's a corker, Seldom, ain't he?"

"A t'orrerbred, Jimmy, a reg'lar outenouter. He don't need no gardeen, he don't."

"D'yer reckon he'll go clean 'round, like he says he's goin?" asked Jimmy presently, when the pair had resumed their recumbent positions on the grass.

"Do I?" responded Seldom, as he lazily blinked at the morning sun. "In course I does. W'y, Jimmy, didn't I say ther kid was er t'orrerbred?" And with this unanswerable retort Seldom Seen pulled down the brim of his rusty hat, and in a few minutes was blending his snores with those of his precious partner.

Meanwhile Paul had been stepping briskly along the track, his heart beating high in anticipation of fresh experiences to be gained in the Mormon capital, his whole frame rejoicing in the contact with the balmy September air, which blew soft and warm, despite the proximity of October.

After the confinement of the preceding days, with its fetid atmosphere, unpleasant quarters and awful jolting, this was like a taste of heaven to the youth, who at times cried aloud in sheer exaltation of spirit and talked such a string of nonsense that anyone overhearing him might have had good reason to question his sanity.

But it was only a natural ebullition following the enforced whispers which for three days had escaped his lips, and if he shouted occasionally to relieve his feelings there was after all nothing extraordinary in such performance.

As the sun rose higher in the heavens Paul's step grew less elastic, and when he had tramped some ten or twelve miles the lad discovered that he was not only very tired, but extremely hungry.

"I'll tackle the next ranch house I spy along the track," was his mental resolve, after fighting off the pains as long as he was able. "Can't get much worse than a refusal anyhow and I'll have to risk that."

Another quarter of an hour and the outlines of a fairly thrifty appearing farmhouse were seen, framed in a grove of timber, about half a mile distant from the railroad.

"Here goes," muttered Paul, as he jumped the ditch that skirted the track. "A hungry stomach has no business to be squeamish, and a dinner of some sort I must have."

Between the railroad track and the house a small bunch of cattle was grazing, and as Paul neared the stock he spied a boy of about fifteen stretched on the prairie intently reading a book.

So interested was the young herder in the story that he failed to notice Paul's approach and started up with a nervous jump when the newcomer, halting within two feet, mildly ventured:

"Say, do you live over yonder?"

"Yep."

"A-h, what time is it?"

"'Bout 'leven o'clock, I guess."

Just then Paul caught a glimpse of the title of the book the lad held in his hand and the interest he felt was perhaps reflected in his voice as he exclaimed, "Swiss Family Robinson, isn't it? How do you like the story?"

"Bully! Far's I've got. Have you read it?"

"Oh, yes, a number of times. They were wonderfully lucky to be wrecked on that island, weren't they?"

The boy darted a keen glance into Paul's face as if he had detected a quizzical note. "Well," he said, "'pears to me they had an awfully smart father. He knew a heap, he did."

"I should say so," assented Paul, and the ice being broken it did not take the young Chicagoan long to establish himself on a very friendly footing with the quick-witted herder, who, after a while, asked Paul to go over to the ranch house for dinner.

This offer was accepted with so much alacrity that both were quick to see the absurdity of the situation and the hearty laugh that burst from each served to clinch their newly formed friendship.

"Didn't think I'd refuse, did you?" questioned Paul, as the two drove the cattle into an adjacent corral.

"N-o. You see I kinder guessed you was hungry when you asked me the time. I knew you wan't a reg'lar tramp, by the way you talked."

Supposing Paul to be some boy acquaintance of Rob, which was the young herder's name, the folks at the ranch house asked no questions and the tired traveler vouchsafed no remarks, particularly as dinner was on the table when the lads entered.

Ah! that was a meal indeed, and the way Paul disposed of the wholesome food was a caution. But as he rose from his chair the thought of a twenty-mile tramp caused him to groan in spirit and he began to wish he had not indulged so freely.

Something of this he expressed to his friend Rob as they sauntered back to the corral.

"Must you go on to Salt Lake this afternoon then?" the latter anxiously inquired.

"Oh, I haven't any pressing engagement," returned Paul. "Why?"

"'Cause if you wait till to-morrow I'll take you up in my buckboard. Mother wants to send some things to my aunt and you can just as well ride with me, if you care to."

"Care to? Why, that will suit me tip-top. But how about a bunk to-night?"

"Oh, that's all right. I have a big bed in the attic all to myself and you can sleep with me."

"It is better to be born lucky than rich," thought Paul, as he closed his eyes that night after indulging in a refreshing bath. "I guess the folks back home haven't forgotten me, either."

The ride through the beautiful valley into town was a rich treat to Paul, whose entertaining conversation seemed to fascinate his younger companion so that they both were fairly sorry when their destination was reached.

By this time Rob had learned Paul's plans, and his interest in the proposed trip was so great that he could talk of little else. He insisted on taking Paul to his aunt's house, and as he was to remain over Sunday entreated his new friend to stay with him.

"But your aunt might object to receiving a stranger," remonstrated Paul, who had some qualms about accepting this generous invitation.

"Oh, no, she won't," urged the boy, "My friends are hers, too. She's jolly good, she is."

And so she was. The best in the house was laid before the lads, for Paul's unaffected manners proved a direct passport to the good woman's heart, and during his stay in Salt Lake her generous hospitality never wavered.

Paul could have found no better guide than Rob, for the young rancher had been born and brought up in the great Salt Lake valley, so that of the two days spent in town not a minute was wasted. All the famous places were visited, including the late Brigham Young's mansion, his tomb, the tabernacle, the great Mormon temple, not then completed, the coöperative stores and the memorable aqueducts where the water refused to run up hill despite the spiritual assurances revealed to the prophet. The beautiful wide streets were duly admired and a drive to Camp Douglas, one of Uncle Sam's most picturesque army posts, brought the lads to the fort in time to witness dress parade at sundown. Last, but not least, came a bath in the Great Salt Lake, an experience that each of the boys hugely enjoyed.

When Monday afternoon arrived the feeling that he had put in his time to the best advantage sent Paul away in a very happy frame of mind, for, true to his original design, he was keen to continue his journey to the west.

"How do you expect to cross the mountains, Paul?" inquired Rob, as they were jogging back to the ranch.

"Haven't any definite plan, yet. I didn't know but Seldom and Jimmy might be able to point out a way," he replied, for Rob had heard all about these queer cronies.

"I have a better scheme than that," remarked Rob, presently, emerging from a brown study. "We used to have a hired man of the name of Jack Turner, who went to braking on the U. P., and I b'leeve he's running on an emigrant train now. If I could catch him going west I know he'd help you, for Jack's a rattling good fellow."

Here was an unlooked-for lead that promised to pan out big, and Paul was soon in a state of feverish anxiety to reach the Union Pacific lest Jack should go through. When Rob explained that Ogden was the end of the division and that Jack lived in town when he was off duty, Paul quieted down, especially as Rob promised to drive over to Ogden first thing in the morning.

Paul's star was still in the ascendant. When the lads reached Ogden next day Jack Turner was almost the first acquaintance Rob greeted. The brakeman chanced to be on his way to the yards to see if the through trains were on time, as he expected to pull out that afternoon.

In response to Rob's earnest request he readily agreed to help Paul out by "fixing" the conductor, so the latter would fail to see him when he went through the train.

"Of course, you understand," said Turner, "that I can only get you passed on to the end of my division, but I'll see if a brakeman I know on the relief crew won't keep you going. Just show up at 2 o'clock and I guess everything will be all right."

Both lads were profuse in their thanks, at which the good-natured brakeman laughingly declared he'd get even by falling back on the ranch for a job if he happened to be laid off any time.

Rob's sincere regard for Paul was made still more apparent when the time for parting arrived. From underneath the seat of the buckboard the boy fished out a market basket tied over with brown paper, which he thrust into Paul's hands, saying: "S'pose you didn't figure that you'd need anything to eat on the road?"

It was an act of thoughtfulness for which Paul was wholly unprepared, and his voice was a bit husky as he stammered his thanks. "If all my experiences are to be as pleasant as this one has been," he said, as soon as he regained his composure, "my tramp will be nothing but a prolonged picnic. Just wait till I get you in Chicago, Rob, and then I'll try to repay some of your many kindnesses."

It was really quite hard to part from the brown-eyed, freckle-faced young Mormon who had proved so true a friend, and Paul found himself speculating as the train sped westward under what circumstances, if ever, they might meet again. But the problem was too deep for instant solution, and before he could arrive at a satisfactory conclusion he was fast asleep.

Jack Turner's "pull" with the new crew was so strong that when he came in the car next afternoon to say goodbye he assured Paul everything would be all right as far as Sacramento, a piece of news that was, of course, most gratefully received.

Meantime Paul had made some acquaintances among the passengers, so that a hot cup of coffee or tea was always forthcoming at meal times.

The car in which Turner had found him a seat was filled with a motley collection of emigrants, most of whom were on their way to southern California. Families predominated, with the usual quota of children, from babies in arms to restless boys and girls of twelve and fourteen.

The confinement in the crowded car had, naturally, tried the patience and temper of both parents and children, so that when Paul entered on the scene the prospect was anything but inspiriting. But with the blissful disregard of surroundings peculiar to a healthy boy, Paul had curled himself up on the seat, after eating his first meal aboard the train, and despite the noise and confusion on all sides, he found no difficulty in wooing the drowsy god.

Next day he had plenty of opportunity to study his fellow travelers at leisure, and it was not long before his cheerful good nature began to assert itself.

The heart of a little woman, whose eldest of three tots was scarcely seven, he gladdened by enticing the youngsters into his seat, where he amused them for upward of an hour by story-telling and propounding mysterious conundrums, which gave the tired mother, traveling to rejoin her husband, a chance to rest for the first time since she had boarded the train.

A fretful child that had cried half the morning he quieted by walking up and down the aisle with the baby perched on his shoulder, until it crowed with delight.

At dusk of the second day the children began to regard Paul as their especial friend, and after their early supper had been discussed he had all the little people in the car crowded into his seat, on his knees, at his back—anywhere within earshot—for Paul could tell the most wonderful fairy stories in a way that held the youngsters spellbound, and their demands for "just one more, please,"

AMUSING THE
EMIGRANTS.

were met until the story teller was too hoarse to continue.

Thus it was that Paul shortly found himself a most popular individual, not only with the children, but with the big folks, too, for since his advent a different sort of atmosphere seemed to pervade the car, and the elders were not slow to perceive the cause. Hence it was not strange that with the approach of meal time three or four invitations were always open to Paul's choice.

At Sacramento many of the emigrants left the train to continue their journey southward, and as Paul met a peremptory challenge for "ticket" from the new conductor, he knew his rope was run, and that he could not hope to get to San Francisco aboard that car. Sadly, but philosophically withal, he said good-bye to his big and little friends, and escorted by a brakeman was piloted through the forward door and ordered to make himself scarce.

Not, however, without having formulated certain definite plans. One of the passengers had advised him to steal aboard one of the river steamers plying between Sacramento and San Francisco and stow away among the cargo. Having at some previous time successfully essayed this trick himself, he further explained how it might safely be accomplished, which so appealed to Paul's imagination that he determined to make the attempt.

With a sandwich resting snugly at the bottom of each outside pocket of his coat, the lad made his way across the gridironed tracks to the wharf, where he remained until dusk awaiting an opportunity to elude the Cerberus at the gate.

As Homer was said to sometimes nod, so also did the vigilance of the guard relax, and at the first good chance Paul slipped inside the gate, bounded lightly across the gangway of a packet moored to the dock, and in a trice had concealed himself among a pile of freight on the lower deck, forward.

Two months before his heart would have beaten like a trip-hammer had he attempted anything so daring as this, and he would probably have remained in a state of constant terror, for fear of discovery.

But now he merely shrugged his shoulders as he lay outstretched across the bags of grain, and with a mental apology to the owners for surreptitiously boarding their vessel, he gazed steadily at the bright moon overhead and actually dropped asleep before the boat left the wharf to steam down the Sacramento River.

As a tramp Paul was making progress.

CHAPTER VI.

A FORTUNE IN EYE-WATER.

ONCE only during the night Paul awoke to find the big moon-eye still beaming above, while the monotonous "chug!" "chug!" of the engine indicated that the boat was keeping steadily on her way down the river.

The next time he opened his eyes it was broad daylight; the vessel was just steaming into her dock, and the clatter all about him told the stowaway that the American continent had been crossed and that San Francisco lay invitingly open to his inspection.

It was no trick to steal ashore unobserved during the bustle contingent on making fast. This safely accomplished the first and most natural question that intruded was how to get breakfast.

"Here, young fellow, want to carry my sample case?" called a gray-bearded drummer at this juncture.

"I'm only going three or four blocks up the street."

With alacrity Paul responded to the hail and quickly fell into line behind the traveling man, whose other baggage consisted of a valise and an umbrella.

Twenty cents—all the small change the man had—Paul received for this service, and with lighter spirits he started in search of a modest restaurant where he might break his fast.

This done he next bent his steps to the post office, where, at the general delivery, three or four fat letters with the Chicago postmark were passed to him through the window.

Outside the big doors, on the front steps of the main entrance Paul eagerly tore open the envelope bearing his mother's familiar handwriting. A quick glance sufficed to assure him all were well at home, and, with a thankful heart, he sat down on the stone coping to leisurely read the letters from his father and sisters.

All were of a like tenor—brimful of love for the wanderer, but anxious for his speedy return. "Surely," wrote

Madge, "you have done enough tramping by this time, and must be about ready to settle down to matter-of-fact life in Chicago. Be a good prodigal and we will promise you the fattest calf in the market."

It was his father only who suspected the true scope of Paul's tramp, and he begged the boy to think twice before putting salt water between him and the shores of America. Yet he placed no limitation on his son's travels, but left the lad free to follow his inclinations, asking in return that he write as often as possible.

It was the last question which Paul ruefully pondered. As to returning to Chicago, why, of course, that was not to be considered—he was only fairly started; but if he could raise money enough to buy stationery and stamps so as to write home he would be moderately happy. That duty must be performed at the earliest opportunity, even if he missed a meal.

From his reverie he was aroused by a smart slap on his back, while a voice in his ear shouted: "Hello, Scotty!"

This familiar salute was given by a

smartly dressed individual, whose sallow features, under a shiny silk hat, were adorned by a luxuriant black mustache. As Paul quickly turned the man saw he had made a mistake, and hastened to apologize.

"Beg your pardon, son. Thought you were a friend of mine from Cincinnati. Had a little job for him and rather expected to meet him here."

Paul took this in good part and smilingly remarked that he bore "Scotty" no ill-will, but he was looking for a job himself.

The man with the mustache ran his eyes over Paul, as if he were mentally "sizing him up." The inspection was evidently satisfactory, for he began to ask a number of questions, and ended by telling the lad to meet him at that same place at 12 o'clock.

The two hours intervening Paul spent in writing letters. Strolling into the Palace Hotel to admire its gorgeous interior, he spied some loose paper and envelopes on one of the writing tables, which had evidently been left by a surfeited guest.

Dropping unconcernedly into the vacated seat, Paul took off his hat, picked up a pen and wrote industriously until nearly noon, unmolested and unchallenged by anyone. At the end of that time he had four bulky letters ready to mail. All he lacked was stamps.

Depositing them in an inside pocket he carelessly meandered out doors, and then walked swiftly to the rendezvous, which he reached just as the clock tolled the noon hour.

Five minutes later his acquaintance of the morning appeared.

"Ah! You're on time, I see," he called, as he mounted the steps. "Well, I admire promptness. Haven't been to dinner, I suppose?"

Paul shook his head,

"Then come along with me, and while we are eating I'll tell you what sort of a job I can offer you."

The unknown led the way to an attractive restaurant on Kearney Street, where he ordered a substantial dinner. During its discussion he explained that his name was Dr. Queechy, and that he was the owner of a wonderful cure for sore eyes that he expected to sell at the state fair at Sacramento, which was to begin next day.

"What I want you to do, Paul," he continued, after the preliminary explanations were over, "is to take charge of my booth at the fair grounds and sell my eye-water to the country visitors. I have the stuff all bottled in pints and quarts, which you may give away at fifty cents and a dollar a bottle."

Paul grinned. "That's a pretty steep price for a countryman to pay, isn't it?"

"Oh, well," returned the doctor, with a fatuous smile, "if it was cheaper the idiots wouldn't touch it at all. It's human nature, my boy. High-priced goods must be extra fine, and, therefore, worth having. You'll see; the stuff'll go off like hot cakes when you get your bills well distributed."

If Paul had any doubts about the merits of Dr. Queechy's lotion they should have been entirely dissipated when he read the sample handbill which the doctor displayed. The wonderful curative properties of the medicine were set forth in no uncertain light, while numerous testimonials from various distinguished citizens vouched for the benefits they had derived from its use. With all this staring him in the face, Paul would have been an ingrate to have doubted, so with a cheery "thank you" he announced his willingness to accept the place.

"All right, then; that's settled," exclaimed the doctor. "Two dollars a day and your expenses. Let's see—train leaves in an hour. Ought to catch that so as to get an early start at the fair to-morrow. Stuff is at the depot; all we have to do is to check it through. Come ahead, son."

On the way to the station Paul pulled out his letters and remarked that he would like to mail them if his employer could make him a small advance on his salary.

The doctor opened his purse and handed his new assistant a silver dollar.

"Would give you more," he said, in his terse, choppy way, "only I'm a little short just now."

Paul protested that ten cents was enough, but the doctor waved him back and told him to say no more about it.

It was a great relief to get the letters off his mind, for Paul's love for his parents was too genuine to allow them to worry through his neglect. As he dropped the envelopes into the box he felt as if that action completed his record up to date. What followed would be a new chapter, which he was only too eager to enter upon.

On arriving at Sacramento their first care was to transfer the bottled goods from the depot to the fair grounds. It was too late to do any work at the booth that night, so the doctor made arrangements for Paul to board at a cheap hotel near by, promising to meet him early the day following at the booth.

By 7:00 o'clock next morning Paul had eaten his breakfast and was off to the grounds. When his employer appeared on the scene the bottles were neatly arranged in pyramids around the octagonal counter, while attractive hangers and flaring dodgers proclaimed the virtues of the lotion in the most effective manner.

"Better get a few small boys to pass around your handbills," advised the doctor, after signifying his approval of Paul's work. "Spend this dollar on it," he added, tossing over the coin, "but wait until the grounds fill up before you set 'em to work. You must stick close to the stand, as I have other business on hand."

Toward noon Paul managed to hire four youngsters at a quarter each, who solemnly promised to scatter the dodgers all over the fair grounds. Apparently their work was honest, for later on he sold half-a-dozen bottles to as many different people, each of whom carried a handbill. By 6:00 o'clock he had disposed of fifteen dollars' worth of eye-water, and as the crowd was then rapidly thinning out, he concluded it was time for him to quit, too. So, locking up his bottles, he closed the booth and went over to his hotel to supper.

Contrary to his expectations, the doctor failed to meet Paul that evening, but, supposing that he would surely receive a visit at the booth in the morning, the lad thought nothing of the omission and went to bed, feeling fairly jubilant over his first day's business.

The second day opened bright and pleasing. The attendance was larger, and, with another judicious distribution of dodgers by his faithful emissaries, sales of eye-water steadily boomed, so that by supper-time Paul's receipts amounted to upward of fifty dollars. Still the doctor did not appear, much to the concern of his assistant, who began to fear some mishap had befallen him.

The day had not passed without bringing many incidents to Paul's notice. Numerous were the questions, both funny and serious, that he was required to answer regarding the efficacy of the eye-water, to all of which the lad replied as truthfully and intelligently as he could.

One old lady, who thought the stuff might possibly help her son Peleg's eyes, wanted to be certain that the medicine would do all that the handbill stated before she invested. Her shrewd questions rather flurried the young salesman.

"You say that 'one bottle will cure the worst case of sore eyes ever known,'" she exclaimed, quoting from the bill she held before her spectacles. "Will you swear to that, young man?"

"Madam, let me explain," answered Paul, deprecatingly. "You see, I cannot swear to it, because I'm only hired to attend this stand, and know very little about the lotion. The doctor is away just now, but he assured me before he left that the medicine would do all he claimed for it. That's all I can tell you."

"Humph! little enough," she grunted. "However, you look honest, boy, so I'll take a bottle, anyway. Peleg's eyes is that bad he can't read out o' the family Bible, which is printed in extry big letters. S'pose them instructions on the bottle tells how to use it, eh? But it's an awful high price to pay, though," she grumbled, as she hobbled off.

They were mostly grangers who bought. It seemed to Paul that a great many farmers were afflicted with ophthalmia in that region, and he wondered if the lotion would make their eyes much worse. Whether the stuff was genuine or a rank humbug, he had no means of telling. He only

SELLING EYE-WATER AT THE FAIR.

had the doctor's word that it was all he represented it to be.

The third day was a repetition, with but slight variation, of the one previous, except that the sales fell off a trifle. The fourth and last day of the fair found the doctor still missing, and so far all Paul's inquiries had been fruitless. In the afternoon, having sold every bottle of eye-water in the booth, and with upward of one hundred dollars in his pocket, he concluded to take a stroll around the grounds in search of the absent one.

It was while describing his employer to one of the fair police that Paul stumbled on his first bit of information concerning the doctor.

"Doctor Quaichy, d'ye call him?" remarked the officer, in a strong Hibernian accent. "Divvle a docther is he, oi don't think. Sure ther feller's as slick a fakir as iver ye seen. Him an' another chap's bin run out o' town for worrkin' a lotthery racket on ther grounds. It's me that's tellin' yer he won't throuble this parrt o' Callifornyer agin for a good bit. Some o' ther lads he bilked lambasted him awful the fust day he opened up and then chased him to the thrain goin' East. Sure he must be nearly to Ne-York be this toime."

This was startling news that might or might not refer to Dr. Queechy. Further investigation, however, convinced Paul that the policeman's story was, in the main, true, for the additional evidence he gathered all pointed to the doctor as the exiled gambler.

What bothered Paul was to know just why his employer had taken so much trouble with the stand. He finally concluded that the gambling had been an after consideration, particularly when he learned that another man had been implicated with him.

After lingering two days in Sacramento to give an account of his stewardship, Paul decided that the doctor either feared to return or else imagined the sale of eye-water hadn't amounted to enough to bother about. There was nothing for him to do but to go back to San Francisco, and with five double eagles wrapped in a chamois bag and visions of the Southern Pacific haunting his active brain, he again turned his face toward the Golden Gate.

His next problem was a knotty one. It was whether to try to reach China and Japan or embark for New Zealand and Australian ports. Regretfully brushing aside thoughts of cute little Japs and pretty musmees, as he realized how helpless he would be in a strange speaking country, without money or friends, he decided that the English colonies would be more suitable for his purpose. It may be that the fact of having an uncle living in South Australia aided him in coming to this determination.

This question settled, the more difficult one of how to get there presented itself. At first Paul supposed it would be an easy matter to ship aboard any of the steamers lying in the harbor, but after spending a day or two in visiting the various vessel agents and captains, he discovered his error.

He wasn't a sailor, cabin boys were out of date and experienced under-stewards were a glut on the market. Evidently there was a conspiracy to turn him down, and with a sigh Paul came to the conclusion that "running away to sea" was more of a fairy tale than a reality, despite all the story books to the contrary.

"Well," thought he, "if I can't ship as a sailor, or get a billet as a steward, I can at least buy a passage as far as my money will carry me. Might just as well spend it this way as any other."

Of the hundred dollars he had about eighty-five left, fifteen having been spent in buying a few necessary articles of clothing, a valise, renting a room and in living expenses. A first class passage to Australia was worth two hundred dollars; by steerage, one hundred dollars. Clearly he could not get that far. To the Sandwich Islands saloon fare was $75; steerage, $30. This was possible, so Honolulu he decided should be his next port of call.

With a philosophy that was open to serious criticism, he next determined to travel first class, arguing that so long as he had money in his pocket he would get the best in sight. Instead, then, of contenting himself with steerage passage and saving the difference, Paul went to the steamship office and rashly engaged a saloon berth to Honolulu.

If he had been a few years older the prospect of landing on an island in the Southern Pacific with but a few dollars in his pocket might have taught him more discretion. As it was he trusted to his usual happy faculty of alighting on his feet, and refused to give any thought for the morrow. Perhaps it was largely owing to his sublime faith in himself that he overcame difficulties which might have appalled a more experienced traveler.

It was on a Thursday morning that Paul planked down his gold twenties on the counter of the steamship office and received in exchange his berth ticket on the City of Sydney. The boat was advertised to sail at 2:00 o'clock in the afternoon. A letter to his father, telling of the step he had taken, another to his mother, and Paul was ready to go on board.

At 5:00 o'clock he was passing through the Golden Gate on his way to the

Sandwich Islands; the Pacific coast was gradually receding and an unknown region lay before him. But the swell was becoming too obtrusive for further reverie on deck, so down to his berth he hurried, with an awful feeling of nausea that stretched him helpless.

When at length he slept, it was to dream that he had married the daughter of a rich planter, and was made prime minister of Hawaii.

CHAPTER VII.

IN THE SOUTHERN PACIFIC.

The City of Sydney was badly crowded. In addition to her regular passenger traffic she carried an American circus troupe, with its accompanying impedimenta, that was going to "do" New Zealand and Australia and, incidentally, the colonials.

The circus pervaded the entire ship. Its trick horses, performing stallions, mules, elephants, camels and other uncaged animals were confined in narrow stalls on the lower deck between the steerage way and amidships, while the fiercer ones, lodged behind iron bars, were scattered up and down the gangways and wherever there was space enough to lash a cage.

The roaring of the lions, hoarse bellowing of the seals, trumpeting of the seasick elephants and other kindred noises emanating from the menagerie, produced a very bizarre effect that first night at sea; hence it was not strange that few passengers slept.

Awakened from his dream of the premiership by the furious trumpeting of a frightened elephant, Paul lay quiet in his bunk for a few minutes until he got his bearings. Then, as a long roller threw the ship over, he felt his stomach rebel, and hastily slid to the cabin floor just as a voice from the lower berth called out, "What's the matter, boy, sick?"

It was the ship's surgeon who asked the question. Pushed for room, the steamship company had even invaded the cabins allotted to the officers, and Paul had been quartered with Dr. Penrose, who had cheerfully consented to the arrangement. It was another instance of Paul's luck, for the jolly doctor was able to do him many a good turn later on.

"I don't feel just right, doctor," responded the lad, as he labored over the basin. "Seems as if I'd lose my toe nails if this keeps up. Oh, dear," he groaned, "guess I wasn't cut out for a sailor," and once more he struggled with his rebellious stomach.

The hard-hearted doctor laughed. "Why, my boy, in another day I'll have you guzzling the fattest piece of fried pork there is in the cook's galley. That's right, let 'er come; you'll be better pretty soon."

Not until there was nothing left to come did Paul feel safe in climbing back into his bunk, and then he was so weak that he quickly dropped to sleep in spite of the bedlamic noises which prevailed.

He told the doctor the next morning that he guessed he'd stick to the cabin for a while, when the latter urged him to get up and eat breakfast; so, promising to send the steward in with a bowl of beef tea and a biscuit, Dr. Penrose left Paul to his meditations.

It wasn't a pleasant morning for the young traveler, and those who have been there themselves will be ready to extend their sympathies. But his was not a very severe attack, and along in the afternoon, by keeping his lips tightly closed, he managed to wriggle into his clothes, and presently found courage to crawl on deck.

There were few passengers promenading. Those who had escaped the prevailing complaint were mostly old stagers who had crossed the ocean so often they had their sea legs with them constantly. There was one notable exception, however, as Paul shortly discovered.

For about an hour he persistently strode up and down the deck, a little white under the eyes and still rather green about the lips, but the awful feeling of nausea had passed away, and with each fresh breath of salt air that he inhaled the lad felt a new invigorating force creeping into his veins.

Oh, but it was glorious to breast the sharp, keen breeze, laden with minute crystals that flecked his cheeks and occasionally lit upon his lips. This was worth all it had cost him so far, he decided, as he rested his arms for a minute on top of the bulwarks and stood watching the dolphins play leap-frog in the briny waves.

Suddenly a smart gust of wind sent the hat of one of the promenaders sailing past the companionway, brought it in collision with a ventilator, lowered it for a second on the skylight over the saloon, and then, picking it up sharply, dashed it full in Paul's face, where its erratic career ended.

It was a Tam o' Shanter of soft, gray wool which Paul grasped and the next minute its owner came beating up into the wind in search of her lost property. She was young—not over sixteen—with merry, laughing eyes, light brown, crisp, curly hair and red, rosy cheeks—a picture of health and youthful beauty.

"Oh, I am so glad you stopped it," she exclaimed, as Paul handed over his prize. "I never expected to get it back again, you know."

Paul smiled and said he was glad to have had the chance of saving her cap from going overboard, and then, as the girl paused to cover her flying locks, he politely called her attention to the dolphins disporting in the water.

She moved close up to the bulwarks and leaned over, the better to look at them.

"What jolly fun they're having down there," she remarked, and by her accent Paul knew she was English. "See how easily they keep up with the ship."

Her companion tried to look down over the rail, too, but his head was hardly equal to the effort, and with a sickly smile he said he guessed he would have to keep moving. "You see, miss," he apologetically explained, "this is my first appearance on deck and I'm not quite used to the motion yet."

Hastily lifting his hat, he started off at a brisk pace, leaving the girl still watching the sportive fish. On his return the second time she started to renew her walk, and the pleasant smile she gave Paul encouraged him to fall in step beside her.

"What a capital sailor you are," he ventured. "This can't be your first trip at sea?"

"Not quite," she replied. "We left Liverpool three weeks ago, so I had a chance to get used to the motion while crossing the Atlantic; but it didn't bother me a bit, even then. Dear mamma was dreadfully ill, though, and stayed in her cabin until we reached New York. I don't suppose we shall see her on deck until we get to Honolulu. Poor Jones, too—that's mamma's maid—is just as bad, so I have to look after myself entirely."

Further conversation with this ingenuous miss revealed the fact that her mamma was the wife of a high official attached to the English embassy at Suva, Fiji, who with her daughter Ethel and the maid, Jones, was on her way to Sydney to meet her husband.

At three bells, or half past five, the lively Miss Ethel announced her intention of going below to dress for dinner, and as by this time Paul had overcome his repugnance for food, he expressed the hope of meeting his new acquaintance in the saloon.

But, as he descended the companionway, he ruefully thought of his one suit of clothes and what a sorry figure he would cut at the dinner table. However, he was too young to let this worry him much, and, after all, with clean linen and a neat four-in-hand tie, he presented a not unattractive exterior.

It was too early in the voyage for

the saloon to be crowded, so Paul found no difficulty in getting a seat near the rosy-faced English lass, who had a good British appetite which nothing seemed to disturb. Considering his recent unpleasant experiences, the young Chicagoan managed to make a very fair meal himself, and between courses mustered up enough ambition to attempt a few responses to the bright sallies of his fair neighbor, whose effervescing spirits were so contagious that Paul had forgotten all about seasickness by the time coffee was served.

It was a very innocent and wholly enjoyable comradeship that the two young people formed for each other during the succeeding days at sea. Just a healthy boy and girl friendship, devoid of any sickly sentimentality. They walked, talked, sung and read together as if they were college chums, and, with no one to interfere with their movements, had a royal good time.

Through the ship they roamed at will, all avenues being open for their inspection. They visited the steerage quarters together, dived down into the fo'castle, made friends with the elephants, chatted with the lion tamer, watched the juggler practice his art on the lower deck, hobnobbed with the side show people, and even discussed amateur photography with the clown, that being his particular hobby.

Card playing, quoit pitching, hop scotch, bean bag, hoop pole, chess, checkers, dominoes, dancing—all the mild diversions calculated to while away the hours on shipboard—they indulged in, the weather meantime proving delightfully fair.

With so charming and congenial a companion it was not strange that the week passed with lightning speed, and Honolulu was in sight almost before Paul realized that the time had arrived when he must say good-by to the ship and his pleasant acquaintances.

Waiting until the last minute before making his adieus, with a heavy heart he left the ship, paid his shore tax of two dollars and then rode up town to the Hawaii Hotel, where he decided to spend the night, cost what it might.

There was a mosquito netting over the bed in his room, but the Kanaka variety of insect laughed it to scorn, and the warm welcome they accorded the stranger when he crept under the canopy was an earnest of the hospitality of the island.

With such bedfellows sleep was banished and after tossing from one pillow to another until daylight, what was left of Paul crawled out of range, hastily dressed and went down to breakfast. When he settled his bill the young traveler found he had just seventy-five cents in cash left, a state of affairs that set him to thinking seriously.

The prospect of being stranded on an island did not please him. Strolling down to the wharf he found the City of Sydney still at her moorings, and, going aboard, incidentally learned from the chief mate that several of the crew had levanted during the night, leaving him short-handed.

A sudden inspiration seized Paul. "See here, Mr. Le Duc, why can't you ship me before the mast? I want to go to Sydney and will gladly sign with you for my passage."

The mate snorted and looked incredulous. "Pretty figure you'd cut aloft in a gale o' wind. I guess not."

But Paul protested so stoutly and stated his predicament so earnestly that the officer weakened and ended by agreeing to transfer his late saloon passenger to the fo'castle as a common sailor.

Half an hour later Paul had actually signed the ship's articles for Sydney, and was soon stowing his valise in a vacant bunk which had been assigned to his use. Doffing his linen shirt, collar and necktie, he again rigged himself out in his tramp attire, and in an hour had reported to the mate for duty.

While helping to take in cargo he kept a sharp lookout for the bright English girl, but as she had gone ashore with her mamma and the maid he was spared all explanations for the present. From his position on the lower deck he saw them drive up to the wharf shortly before the boat cast off, and with curiously mixed feelings watched Ethel and her mamma, half buried under gay flowers, trip across the gang plank, followed by Jones bearing a large bunch of bananas.

A lump rose in his throat as he

realized there was now a sharp line drawn between them that would effectually end further intercourse, and he dreaded the hour when they must meet. He found himself speculating how his former jolly comrade would act when she encountered him at work scrubbing the deck or engaged in some such menial labor. Shrugging his shoulders, he reflected that it was only a part of his experiences, and his native philosophy again came to his aid.

Paul was assigned to duty with the port watch, and by the time he had served a week before the mast he was thoroughly imbued with the deep religious convictions Dana experienced when he sailed around Cape Horn. The same sentiment pervaded the City of Sydney. It was:

Six days shalt thou labor and do all thou art able,
And on the seventh—holystone the main deck and scrape the cable.

Paul's efforts at "sailoring" were confined chiefly to scrubbing the deck, cleaning paintwork, polishing brass ornamentation and shifting cargo in the hold, all of which was pretty hard manual labor to the tenderly-reared youth.

But he never shirked his duty nor shrank from it, no matter how distasteful the work. He had one solacing thought that kept him ever cheerful. He knew the discomforts were but temporary, and was prepared for a stoical endurance until the ship reached Sydney harbor.

The hardest task to which the embryo sailor was assigned was in handling cargo in the ship's hold on hot afternoons, when the thermometer registered anywhere from 90 to 110 degrees. The youngest and slimmest of any in his watch, he was expected to work alongside the toughest old stagers and still make as good a showing as they.

Stripped to the waist and perspiring at every pore, he would yet manage to compress his lips into a grim smile and try to think that in another month the agony would be over and he would be laughing in real earnest.

Sometimes his back ached so frightfully and his tongue was so dry and parched that he felt he must drop in his tracks before the hour of relief arrived. But he was too proud to complain, and by gritting it through he became gradually inured to the rough service.

When resting in his bunk, after such spells, he decided that the lad who is dissatisfied with his home and yearns to become a sailor has only to ship aboard an ocean steamer for a voyage to the South Pacific to have the nonsense knocked out of him. One trip, he thought, would be sufficient unless the lad were made of extra stern stuff.

Perhaps Paul's severest test came when he was first sent aloft. It was the second night out from Honolulu. Going on deck at eight bells, midnight, he was ordered up with the rest of the watch to furl the sails, which strong headwinds rendered useless.

A small sized gale was blowing above, and the glance Paul threw upward sent his heart into his boots. He looked around for a hiding-place, and found it behind a coil of rope, which hung from a belaying pin. Just as he was disappearing in the gloom, the second mate's voice rang out:

"You young scamp, come out o' that, or I'll skin ye alive. Hump yourself, now."

The culprit meekly crawled forth.

"Now, then, jump into them shrouds, unless ye want the toe o' my boot along yer spine. No skulking here. Pile up there in a hurry!"

Paul stole a glance at the mate—the "little bulldog," the sailors had dubbed him—noted his heavy sea-boots and concluded to follow the rest of the port watch. With his heart in his mouth he sprang into the rigging and slowly and cautiously made his way into the maintop.

Here the sailors lay along the yard taking in canvas, and when they saw the greenhorn creeping along the foot-rope they gave him a characteristic reception.

"Hang on with your eyebrows, Johnny!"

"Bet he's glued to the ropes!"

"Somebody throw him a fishline!"

"Put a half hitch 'round him!"

It was good-natured banter, if a trifle

rough, but the lad paid little attention to it, for meantime the wind was whistling about his ears and singing a tune in them that might as well have been a dirge, for Paul never expected to get back alive. However, he kept his teeth tightly shut and doggedly took up a position on the precarious footrope, which seemed like packthread to his excited imagination.

Over the boom he bent, and with one hand grasping the jackstay employed his right in scooping in sail. Still higher up was another portion of the crew taking in the main-top-gallant-sail, but for a first attempt Paul concluded he had done enough, and he had no ambition to join them. Waiting until all the sails were neatly furled, he crawled out to the end of the yard and began the descent.

As he had scorned to take advantage of the lubber's hole in ascending he gave it as wide a berth going down and bravely swung himself into the futtock shrouds until his body assumed the shape of a right-angled triangle. For a moment he hung in space; then his feet caught the ratlines and his hair began to resume its normal condition. With his heart beating like a trip-hammer he reached the lower shrouds, and jumped to the deck, where he leaned heavily against the bulwarks to steady himself.

But the "bulldog" was laying for him.

"Hello! Skulkin' again, eh?" exclaimed the mate, catching sight of Paul's trembling figure. "Blast my buttons if I don't knock that foolishness! Get a bucket o' hot water and a scrubbin' brush and report to me lively."

The remainder of the night Paul spent in scrubbing paintwork on the bridge, his efforts being expedited by constant growls from the vicious mate, who seemed to take a keen delight in worrying the lad.

The youngster was buying his experience pretty dearly these days.

CHAPTER VIII.

ABOARD THE CITY OF SYDNEY.

AFTER that first trip to the upper regions Paul rather enjoyed the order to "lay aloft." Being light and active his station was at the extreme end of the yard on the main-to'-gallants'l. Here, resting on the footrope and grasping the jackstay, he would stand and look down on the deck, which, from that height, appeared like the back of a huge snake wriggling through the water. With so much weight above it seemed impossible for the ship to maintain her equilibrium while plowing through the waves. Sometimes he would close his eyes and try to believe the boat was keeling over, but she always righted when he opened them again.

It was inevitable that the bright little English girl should, sooner or later, discover Paul's identity in the young sailor whose duties often called him to that portion of the deck abaft the wheelhouse held sacred to saloon passengers.

As a matter of fact his story had already been discussed at the saloon table. One of the circus performers, having noticed the lad's resemblance to their former fellow passenger, chanced to mention the circumstance in the presence of the mate, who, of course, explained away the mystery. Gossip in restricted quarters spreads rapidly, any incident is news on shipboard, so that Paul's sudden transposition furnished material for speculation to the entire cabin. Some sympathized with the youngster's ambition to see the world; a few expressed the opinion that he would better be at steady work, while several hinted significantly that perhaps the young scapegrace had good reasons for leaving America. Uncharitable people like the latter are always to be met, but fortunately they are in a blessed minority. Those who had been on speaking terms with the lad were prompt to reject a suggestion so palpably absurd and unjust.

In Miss Ethel Paul unconsciously

found a warm defender. Someone in her hearing having referred slightingly to her quondam companion, with the fearlessness of youth she rebuked the speaker and stoutly resented the implied slur.

It was shortly after a discussion of this nature that his champion met Paul face to face as the latter stood coiling ropes' ends around their respective belaying pins on the starboard quarter, aft.

Four or five days had elapsed since Honolulu had been left behind and this was their first meeting. Several times Ethel had been on the point of speaking to her former acquaintance, but Paul had always evaded her approach. It was now impossible to avoid her without appearing positively rude.

"You don't know how astonished I was to find you back here again," she exclaimed in a breath, as if anxious to save him any explanations; "but I am sure it's all right and I'm awfully glad you didn't stay in Honolulu."

"You are very kind, Miss Ethel," he murmured, keeping his eyes fixed on the rope he continued coiling. "The truth is," he blurted, suddenly meeting her sympathetic gaze, "I'm trying to see a bit of the world, and as my money gave out I started in to work my way as far as I could."

"And quite proper, too, I am sure."

"That's what I thought. It isn't so very easy," he confessed, half laughingly, "and not nearly so pleasant as when I was a passenger, but I don't mind it now I'm getting used to the work. How is your mamma? Does she still keep to her cabin?"

"Oh, my, yes; and Jones, too. Captain Dearborn threatened this morning to have them both carried on deck by force if they didn't try to get up, but, of course, he was only joking. You don't know how I miss our walks and talks," she added, wistfully.

"You are very good to say so, Miss Ethel," returned Paul, as he threw the last coil over the pin where it belonged. "I wish—but no, what's the use of wishing. It will be a pleasant thought always, though, to know that you enjoyed our short acquaintance." Then, as he spied the form of the second mate coming toward them, he hastily doffed his hat, and crossed to the port side, where more uncoiled ropes awaited his dexterous manipulation.

The second mate still had it in for Paul, and took it upon himself to make life on shipboard as burdensome as possible to the lad. When he was in charge of the deck Paul was sure to get the meanest and most obnoxious duties assigned to him, regardless of his adaptability to the work, and if everything did not prove satisfactory the young sailor was deluged with curses by way of reward for his pains.

These unpleasant attentions became so marked that the usually unimpressionable sailors forming the port watch declared the little bulldog took a special dislike to Paul because he was a gentleman. Among themselves he was simply "Chicago," the only title by which they addressed him, and that he was a general favorite with all was proof positive that the attitude of the second mate was wholly unwarranted.

So far Paul had been able to maintain a perfectly respectful exterior toward his tyrant, although on several occasions he was sorely tempted to rebel. But his philosophy had nerved him to accept the situation meekly, and he had determined that nothing should induce him to talk back.

But there are limits to one's most patient endurance, as Paul was fated to discover. Scarcely had he begun to coil the tangled ropes that lay on the port deck when the bulldog bore down upon him.

"What were you chinning that girl for?" he demanded, in his most insolent manner.

A quick retort sprang to the lad's lips, but repressing it by an effort, he deliberately turned his back on the little bully and grimly stuck to his task.

His attitude was so contemptuous that the mate could not fail to interpret it aright, and his bile rose instantly.

"You young whelp!" he shouted. "D'you think you were hired to loaf away time by spinning fairy tales to the passengers? Just keep your monkey tongue to home or I'll shove you down in the lazarette for a few days to teach you manners. You can't play the sympathetic dodge on this boat while I'm around."

If Paul could have annihilated the fellow with a look the hot glance he flashed at him would have shriveled the mate in his tracks. So far he had let all insults pass unnoted, but this miserable insinuation made him very angry. Furious with rage, he turned savagely on his tormentor. "You coward," he hissed, "if I had you on shore and you were ten times my size I'd lick you for that if I died doing it. But I've stood all I'm going to take from you anyway, mister, so just keep your hands off."

The worm had turned. Paul confronted his enemy with a mien so undaunted that it told the officer he had made a mistake. The sturdy, well-knit youngster, for all his soft skin and smooth-spoken ways had plenty of grit. As he stood there with the half-coiled rope quivering in his left hand, his right fist hanging clinched by his side, and his face blazing with honest indignation, he presented a striking contrast to the scowling mate, who, after muttering some unintelligible threats, turned on his heel and walked rapidly toward the bridge.

Angry as he was, Paul could not help laughing to see the sulky humor displayed by the little bulldog as he went snarling away. But he mentally vowed that he would hold no further conversation with the saloon passengers. It hurt his pride to be accused of seeking sympathy.

Next morning was Sunday, and the day was ushered in by a funeral. Not of a human being, but of a favorite black performing stallion belonging to the circus, which had died during the night. Its trainer shed real tears as the inert form of his pet was hoisted over the side, and even the hardy sailors felt a sympathetic throb as the glossy hide of the dead brute struck the water with a great splash and was swallowed up by the waves. The white belly of a shark was seen as it rushed toward its prey, and Paul had an uncomfortable twinge as he realized how easily the latter might have been a passenger or one of the crew instead of a dumb animal.

Down in the fo'castle Sunday was

devoted to the repairing of wardrobes, washing of clothing, haircutting, shaving, bathing and other personal affairs, which a partial respite from cargo shifting, paint cleaning and brass polishing rendered possible. Lying in his bunk, watching the wreaths of cigarette smoke that were puffed up by the swarthy Spaniard below him, Paul half forgot the indignities to which he had been subjected, and for a few hours listened with drowsy delight to the yarns spun by the heterogeneous mixture that composed the crew of the City of Sydney.

A careless, godless gathering of the restless element of all nations. Scandinavian, Finn, Spaniard, Italian, French, English, German and Greek, with a whaler or two from New Bedford and several fresh-water sailors from the big inland lakes; grumbling constantly, as is their wont, yet ready in an instant to face the dirtiest weather that ever fell to the lot of a navigator. Good enough fellows of their kind, but a kind that was not the best in the world for an impressionable lad to become intimate with. Luckily the companionship was not to continue long enough to leave any lasting ill effects on Paul.

Sunday dinner for the cabin passengers was usually a swell affair, and as the appetizing odor from the saloon galley seeped into the fo'castle Paul could not help an involuntary sigh for the fleshpots of Egypt, as he thought of their own regulation "salthorse" and the pale slabs of bilious pudding, known as "plum duff," thrown in by way of Sunday dessert. Fo'castle fare palled on his palate for the time being.

When the port watch went on duty that evening there was a fair wind and little to do except laze around and wait for orders. While resting in the shadow of the engine room Paul felt a light touch on his elbow, and the musical voice of the English lassie suddenly recalled him from dreams of home. Before he could stammer a refusal she had thrust into his hands half a dozen oranges that she took from a black silk bag and which she ordered Paul to slip inside the loose tennis shirt he wore.

"But, Miss Ethel," he protested, "I really can't permit you to—"

"Hush, sir, not a word," was the half laughing, half imperious retort. "I bribed the pantryman to get these for me, and you must take them or I shall feel hurt. Here are some nuts and raisins, too, so hold open your pockets," and regardless of Paul's deprecations the warm-hearted girl emptied the bag of its contents.

"All right, since you insist," he said resignedly; "but I claim the privilege of dividing the spoils with my watch."

"Do as you please, only take them," she answered lightly, and with a merry laugh and a cordial good-night disappeared in the gloom.

The port watch had its full share of the plunder from the cabin table and asked no questions. The sailors accepted what was given without caring to know how it was obtained, and in doing so displayed a true philosophical spirit worthy of the craft. Nor was that their only feast, for the week following, on six successive nights, the black silk bag came up loaded from the cabin and its burden was duly transferred to Paul's capacious tennis shirt.

During this time the little bulldog had refrained from openly blackguarding Paul, but he never failed to evince his hostility to the lad by assigning him to the most onerous tasks whenever he was on duty. Once he happened along just as Paul was distributing the night's plunder among his fellow sailors, but they scattered quietly and apparently escaped detection.

It was shortly after this that the big fruit box on the main deck just aft of the engine room was broken open during the night and a quantity of bananas and other edibles abstracted. The crew was subjected to a rigid examination, but nothing incriminating was proved and inquiry had about subsided when the second mate, with a malignant grin, asked one of the sailors who gave him the fruit that he had seen him surreptitiously eating on several consecutive nights while on watch.

The man was staggered and tried to evade the question, but the mate was persistent and the story of Paul's generosity had to be disclosed. The bo's'n was instantly dispatched to find the youngster, and, with the little bulldog as his accuser, Paul was promptly haled before the first mate to explain his conduct and to tell how and when he obtained the fruit.

"It was given me on several different occasions by one of the cabin passengers," was the reply.

"Which passenger?"

"I prefer not to give the name."

"But you must if you expect me to believe such a yarn," exclaimed the mate contemptuously.

"I am very sorry, Mr. Le Duc," said Paul, feeling how hopeless this rendered his case, "but, indeed, I cannot tell you."

"Then, sir, I am compelled to think that you are lying and a thief to boot. Bo's'n, lock him up in the lazarette until Captain Dearborn decides what shall be done."

The lazarette was a dark hole on the deck below the saloon cabin, a stuffy compartment, where the liquor was stored and where big, gray rats held high revel. Into this dismal, illy-ventilated hold Paul was rudely thrust and left to commune with his thoughts, his only protection against utter darkness being a tallow candle set in a horn lantern which swung from a beam overhead.

Arming himself with a stave to repel unpleasant boarders, Paul climbed on top of a barrel of rum, and, drawing up his knees, fell to pondering his position.

The situation was dubious, he had to confess, and the chances for proving his innocence appeared slim. With a deep sigh he reflected that he could not expect his good luck to last forever, and must prepare for the other kind, which he knew was bound to overtake him sometime. Of course there was a way of clearing himself, but he instantly rejected the notion of divulging the name of his fair benefactor. Better rats and misery than be guilty of so scurvy a trick as that, he decided.

Eight long, weary hours he passed in the foul-smelling lazarette, with only one caller from the outside world, who left a pannikin of water and some hard bread for the prisoner's diet. There were plenty of other callers, though, from within; big fellows, with black, beady eyes and ugly-looking teeth, whose eager, hungry looks made Paul's flesh creep. But the vigorous manner in which he handled the barrel stave kept the rats at a respectful distance, and so long as the lantern held out to burn he was safe from attack.

But the candle sunk lower and lower in its socket, and Paul's heart was correspondingly depressed as the prospect of total darkness insinuated itself. Nerved to desperation, he began to search around the lazarette and at length discovered three candle stumps tucked away in a crevice, which the rats had been unable to reach. Overjoyed at his find he bore his precious prizes back to the barrel and then grimly waited while the candle in the lantern slowly melted away. But before it sputtered out he caught the dying gleam, and in the still warm socket inserted the first of his fresh supply.

Three times the lone watcher deftly made the transfer of his candle stumps, and Paul could not help thinking that the operation was a good deal like sitting up with one's own corpse. But what next? His last candle end was now burning, and only an inch or so remained between him and the horrible darkness. He tried to shout, but the low ceiling flung back all sound and showed him the futility of his efforts.

Then, for the first time since leaving home, his nerve failed him, and, burying his face in his hands, the poor boy groaned in misery. Presently a scuffling among the refuse at the base of the barrel recalled his wandering senses, and, with an exclamation of disgust, Paul awoke to life and renewed courage in time to aim a quick blow at a big, saucy rat that was making desperate leaps to reach the silent figure on the barrel.

Just as the candle was expiring and odd shadows were chasing each other around the compartment the door of the lazarette was thrown back and the bo's'n's voice called: "Hello, Chicago!"

"Aye, aye, sir."

"Cap'n wants you on deck."

Down slid Paul from his perch, and in two seconds he had scrambled up the short steps to the fresher air above. Filling his lungs as he followed his guide, he presently emerged on the upper deck, where the cool night wind singing through the shrouds made sweetest music in his ears.

Captain Dearborn received him brusquely but kindly. "Look here, my lad," he said, "we have found the real thief that broke open the fruit bin, which, of course, exonerates you. I have also learned where your supply came from. The young lady has been to see me and explained everything. I am sorry that you were placed in durance, but, as you know, the evidence was against you. Now go and turn in and report for duty in the morning."

"Very good, sir," replied Paul, somewhat mystified. "But, if you will excuse me, captain, surely Miss Eth— that is—you don't mean to say the young lady is the culprit?" and his looks of consternation were a study.

The skipper broke into a hearty laugh. "Well, no, hardly that. Perhaps it is only fair to tell you that some of the passengers—two of the circus troupe, in fact—drank more wine than was good for them last night, and in

DOWN IN THE
LAZARETTE.

a crazy freak looted the fruit bin. They very promptly owned up to it when they learned one of the crew had been charged with the theft. Then came the young lady to tell of her share in forging the chain of evidence, after which I sent for you at once. Better say nothing about this," he added, as Paul stepped back toward the door. "The bo's'n will explain that you are innocent."

"All right, sir, I'll remember," returned Paul, saluting as he withdrew. But as he walked slowly toward the fo'castle he thought a little bitterly of the horrors of the last few hours; of the search for candles; of his agony lest the light should fail; of the black, beady eyes and sharp teeth of the rats, and of the unjustness of it all. Then he turned in; but his sleep was troubled, for a procession of monster rats chased across his pillow all night long.

CHAPTER IX.

FOLLOWING THE RED WAGON.

Of course no more fruit from the cabin table found its way into the fo'castle. Even if the inclination remained, the opportunity was lacking, for a spell of bad weather succeeded the long, unbroken run of pleasant sailing, rendering the deck anything but attractive to the passengers.

Once only Paul and the rosy-cheeked English lass met before Auckland was sighted. It was after a steady downpour lasting twenty-four hours, which had kept everybody immured below deck. Chafing under the confinement, the girl had slipped on her London goloshes, donned her mackintosh, and stolen out of the stuffy saloon for a breath of fresh air above. She passed Paul as he crouched under the lee of the port lifeboat, and at first did not recognize the young sailor clad in dripping oilskins, who touched the brim of his sou-wester as she scudded along.

"Oh, dear, is that you—Paul?" she stammered, with a pretty hesitancy. "I have so wanted to see you. I think it was just splendid in you not to tell. I did not hear of the broken fruit bin until long past dinner-time, and then only by the merest accident learned that you were suspected and had been put in that horrid lazarette. I felt sure you hadn't said a word to Captain Dearborn about my giving you the fruit, so I went to see him immediately. Gracious, how he scolded," she exclaimed, with an expressive shrug. "But I didn't mind that, for he promised to send the bo's'n to get you instantly. He told me the circus men had just owned up to what they had done, but said I mustn't say anything about it, as it was a foolish piece of business. Did he tell you I had talked with him?"

"Yes, indeed, and"—here Paul looked rather foolish—"do you know, I came near making a horrible blunder? The captain hadn't said a word about the circus fellows, but after telling me the real culprit had been found he remarked that you had called on him and confessed everything. Well, for a minute I thought he meant you had committed the burglary. You should have heard him laugh when I declared it was impossible. Then he explained more clearly and sent me off to my quarters. But it was very good of you to go to him, Miss Ethel," declared Paul, earnestly, "and I have anxiously looked for a chance to tell you how deeply I appreciate it."

"Nonsense," she retorted. "It would have been despicable had I kept silent, and I should have hated myself ever after. It is I, not you, who am indebted, and I shall never, never forget it." Then, with characteristic impulsiveness, she held out both hands toward Paul, and after leaving them in his firm grasp for a brief moment, suddenly snatched them loose and darted away into the mist, and, as he felt, out of his life forever.

As was natural, Paul had come in contact with quite a number of the circus people since his advent "before the mast," from the "main guy," as the proprietor was known, down to the humblest animal attendant. The knowledge that the troupe intended to make a tour of New Zealand before visiting the mainland of Australia had filled him with a strong desire to see the islands also. To hire out to the circus in some capacity had been his fixed purpose from the day they left Honolulu, but until the fruit-bin incident he had been unable to get any encouragement.

His manly attitude on that occasion was bruited around among the troupe and proved an open sesame to the jolly Irish-American who controlled the Great American Consolidated Arenas. Word came to Paul soon after that if he happened to be in the vicinity of the show grounds when the big tent went up at Auckland he would be taken care of by the manager.

To quit the ship at Auckland was his firm resolve. The little bulldog continued to make things so unpleasant for him that at times he felt wicked enough to steal up behind his tormentor and push him overboard. Luckily he always managed to resist this inclination, but after each fresh indignity he was more than ever determined to break away at the first opportunity.

Perhaps the second mate divined the intention of the young sailor, for, as the ship steamed into the Auckland harbor, he ordered the bo's'n's mate to keep his weather eye on the lad, who, having signed articles for Sydney, was amenable to discipline if detected in an attempt to "jump the ship."

One of the sailors in the port watch, chancing to overhear the mate's instructions, warned Paul to be on the lookout, and suggested that he throw the little bulldog off the scent by waiting until all the paraphernalia of the circus was unloaded on the wharf before he made a move. This advice was so good that Paul concluded to profit by it, so instead of trying to steal away the first night, as he originally intended, he turned out next morning at daylight to bear a hand in unloading, and for the rest of the day worked almost under the nose of his persecutor.

The ruse was successful. His suspicions lulled, the little bulldog relieved the bo's'n's mate from further espionage, and that very night Paul slung his valise over his shoulder, shinned down a rope that hung over the vessel's side, dropped like a cat on the wharf, and quietly disappeared in the direction of the town.

Snugly hidden in a convenient lodging house which commanded a view of the shipping, Paul did not venture forth until the City of Sydney had cast off her mooring ropes and was steaming out into the ocean again. Then, safe from all pursuit, he quickly made his way to the circus grounds, where the "boss" canvasman was marking out the pins for the big tent.

"Hello, Chicago!" was the greeting he received. "How did you manage to break away?"

"French leave," returned Paul, laconically.

"Want to go to work?"

"Sure thing."

"Grab a sledge, then, and join that gang over yonder; you'll get all the exercise you want with this outfit."

Paul selected a light sledge-hammer from the pile indicated, and, slinging it across his shoulder, trudged to the north end of the grounds, where five men, under the direction of the assistant boss canvasman, a tall freckled-faced young fellow called "Redney," were driving stakes.

Redney grinned as the lad approached. "Made it all right, didn't ye?" he said. "Well, git a move on yer and edge in here."

The gang widened and made a space for the newcomer. Circled around a fresh stake pin the first man tapped it into an upright position; after which each hammer fell in rapid sequence until the billet was driven home, and, Redney calling "belay," the squad passed on to the next pin.

This was Paul's introduction to circus life. It was some days before he became adept at slinging a sledge, and many a time he missed the pin and broke the continuity of blows by coming down on his neighbor's hammer. But he had been putting on muscle down in the hold of the City of Sydney and his hard labor there now served him an excellent turn.

The boss canvasman was right when

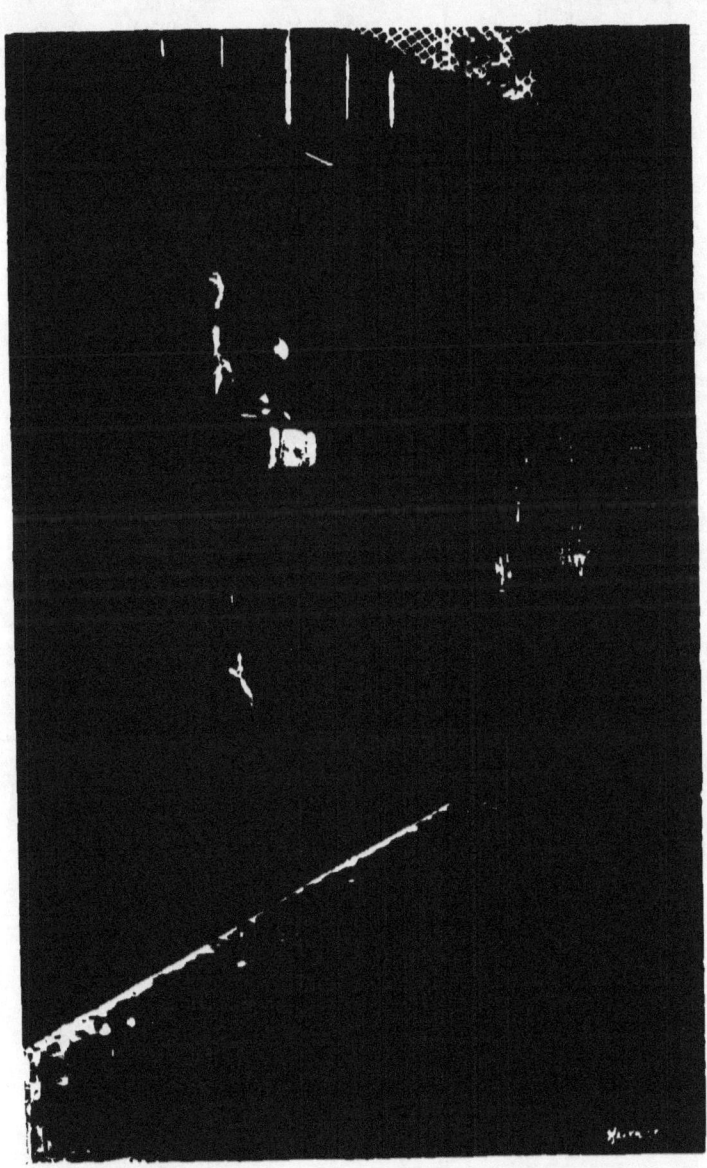

ESCAPING FROM
THE SHIP.

he told Paul he would get all the exercise he wanted. The canvas hands were worked like horses and treated with even less consideration than is usually accorded dumb animals. The majority, however, were but little better than brutes. A drinking, thieving lot of men, homeless, friendless and destitute of any self-respect, with a sprinkling of the greatest rascals that ever cheated justice. For weeks they had awaited the coming of the circus, which had been extensively billed in advance, and the tougher the applicant the more likelihood of his being employed.

This was the sort of society in which Paul mingled for the next ten days following his connection with the show. But in the second week of his engagement the property man chanced to take a fancy to Paul's active figure, and with the consent of the boss canvasman the lad transferred his allegiance to the "dressing room," where he came into more intimate relations with the stars of the arena—the leapers, tumblers, bareback riders, clowns, contortionists, trapeze performers and conjurers.

The "dressing room" was a wall tent, a trifle the worse for wear, divided into two compartments by a strip of canvas, on either side of which the male and female members of the troupe disrobed and "made up" for the ring. Across this flimsy barrier the star actors flung jokes and exchanged repartee during the process of dressing, and in one corner of the tent Paul was initiated into the secret of balloon making—those flat, tissue-paper, circus affairs with which every American boy and girl is so familiar.

His ship name stuck to him. He was "Chicago" to everybody from the day he hired out to the show, and as "property boy" he was at the beck and call of everyone who had the run of the dressing room. But in spite of the drudgery, the snubs and indignities, Paul actually enjoyed the new condition of things. This was seeing life in earnest, and if being behind the scenes took away much of the glamour of the ring, it added largely to the lad's experience.

Paul possessed the happy faculty of forgetting unpleasant things quickly. He saw and heard a great deal that was not calculated to elevate him either mentally or morally during the three months he traveled with the circus, and yet it is doubtful if his sense of right and wrong was in the slightest degree blunted by his temporary affiliation with the show people.

The troupe remained nearly three weeks at Auckland, with audiences packed clear to the ring. The day before the circus was to sail for Wellington Paul was taken with a raging headache, and by the time the night performance was over he was burning up with a fever. Heroic doses of quinine served to check the latter, but the pain in his head continuing, some one suggested a dose of chloral, which the lad swallowed unquestioningly.

Through a stupid blunder on the part of the chemist the quantity given was largely in excess of the regulation amount, so that next day when the Rotomahana was ready to sail his circus friends carried Paul on board still unconscious. Of that short voyage along the New Zealand coast to the capital of the north island the poor boy knew nothing, nor had he recovered his senses when the troupe disembarked at Wellington.

There were subdued voices in the room adjacent when Paul finally awoke to a consciousness of his surroundings. He lay perfectly still for a long time, trying to decide where he was, and by what means he had reached quarters so unfamiliar. The room was evidently in a hotel, that was apparent from the meager appointments. Had the troupe left him behind at Auckland, or was this Wellington? If the latter, how did he get there?

Still drowsy from the effects of the drug, he closed his eyes and was drifting away again when the door between the two rooms was pushed open, and a female voice, which he recognized, recalled his wandering senses.

"Isn't it singular, Jenny, that the boy doesn't wake up? Dick called in a doctor to see him, and he said that there was no danger, but I declare I don't like the looks of it, do you?"

"Why, it is queer," assented the

other, whom Paul knew as one of the women riders, "but why wasn't he left at Auckland, Fanny?"

"Oh, Dick took a fancy to him. He said it was a shame to leave him behind among strangers, so he guaranteed to stand all expenses, and asked the 'old man' to let him come along with us. Just look at the boy's face, Jen; he's from a pretty good family, I know. Wonder why he left his home?"

"Yes, and haven't you noticed how well he talks, too. The boys say he ran away from his folks to go around the world. Do you suppose they have any idea where he is? What's his real name, Fanny?"

"Paul Travers, I believe; his people live in Chicago. Dick found a letter from the boy's father, and he says he'll write to the old gentleman if the young one doesn't get better soon. No use scaring him, though, without any need for it."

The door was closed and the voices became inaudible. Thoroughly awake, Paul recollected with a sensation of relief that he had mailed two letters home the second day after reaching Auckland. He felt very thankful that Dick had not yet written to his father.

Dick Baxter, or, as he appeared on the circus bills, "Leonard Trevylian," the wire-rope bicycle rider, was one of the star attractions. His wife did a clever "manege act" also, besides singing in the concert at the close of the regular performance. He had gone out of his way on one or two previous occasions to do Paul a good turn, and now, it appeared, he was instrumental in bringing him to Wellington. A single salty tear fell on his cheek as Paul dwelt on this last kindness to an almost total stranger. Thinking of it helped him to throw off the lethargy, and with a great effort he opened his eyes again and sat up in bed.

He was only partially undressed. His hat, coat and shoes lay on a chair by the washstand. Nerving himself to the attempt, Paul crawled out of bed and started across the uncarpeted floor to reach them. But he had overestimated his powers; the room spun before his eyes and he sunk in a nerveless heap just as the hall door opened, and his friend Dick, entering, exclaimed: "What are you trying to do, kid?"

"Get up," murmured the boy.

"Yes? Well, don't be in too much of a sweat," was the playfully sarcastic response. "You sneak back into bed again until you've had a square meal inside of you. D'ye know how long you've been asleep?"

"I can't imagine," returned Paul, dropping thankfully across the foot of the bed, "but I know you have been very kind to me."

"Oh, pshaw! that's nothing. But what do you think of sleeping seventy-two hours at a stretch without waking once? That's the kind of a trick you've been up to."

"Seventy-two hours without waking?" Paul repeated in bewilderment. "Is it possible?" Then after a minute's thought he exclaimed: "Ah! It must have been the medicine they gave me. It was too strong, I guess."

"Well, yes, rather," said Dick dryly. "Took enough to put the big elephant, Queenie, to sleep. Lucky thing you had a good constitution, or it's goodbye, Mister Chicago, that trip."

Paul smiled feebly and again expressed his gratitude to his good friend for what he had done. But Dick cut short further remarks by hastening downstairs to order a bowl of beef tea and other nourishing food for his patient.

Paul's recovery was rapid. Two days later he was back at the circus filling his former assignment of balloon-making and in a week had fully regained his accustomed strength.

One morning, about three days after the Wellington engagement expired, Paul found the ringmaster fretting under a bad dilemma. Dick Baxter, the bicycle rider, whose act was billed as one of the star performances, was suddenly attacked by typhoid fever, and a substitute had to be procured in order to keep faith with the colonials. In this case it was not so easy to provide an understudy, as the bicyclist's act was to ride across a wire rope stretched from pole to pole some forty or fifty feet above the ring.

The grooved wheel he sat was held

in position by two trapeze performers, whose combined weight maintained the equilibrium of the machine. It was Dick's custom, when the center of the ring was reached, and amid the breathless suspense of the audience, to stand on his head on the saddle of the wheel, the gymnasts preserving a rigid immobility below during the progress of the thrilling scene.

Aside from this daring feat it was not much of a trick to work the treadles, but it required considerable nerve to climb to that height and calmly submit to the jars and joltings of the trapeze performers, whose gyrations swayed the fragile wheel clear out of perpendicular every time they moved.

In vain the ringmaster begged and bullied the leapers and tumblers to essay the feat. Each one he adjured flatly refused to entertain the proposition for a minute, although, as he explained, he did not expect them to stand on their heads, but simply to ride the wheel. Finally one of the leapers jokingly cried: "Why don't you ask 'Chicago' to do it? He's used to going aloft."

The ringmaster in despair turned to him. "How is it, Chicago? do you want to ride the wheel for me until Dick gets well?"

"I wouldn't mind trying it, sir, on one condition."

"What's that?"

"If you'll agree to pay Dick his salary right along."

The ringmaster thought a minute. "I'll do it," he said. "We're going to move Dick to a private hospital this afternoon, and his wife will stay behind to nurse him until he is able to join us. He shall be taken care of all right."

"It's a go, then; I'll try it," was Paul's quiet response.

"Very good; we'll have a rehearsal in an hour, or as soon as the stallions have been worked. Meantime you and the Kelseys talk it over."

The Kelseys were brother and sister. They were the two who performed on the trapeze, which, affixed to the wheel, hung below the wire rope. Both assured the lad there wasn't a particle of danger if he kept cool and that all he had to do was to sit firmly in the saddle and work the treadles while they did their "act" underneath.

They explained how he was to get on the wheel after they were in position, their weight insuring the perpendicularity of the machine and reducing the danger to a minimum. For like reasons he was to get off first when the performance was over, and stand on the platform, so they could descend together to receive the plaudits of the relieved audience in proper style.

When the hour had expired Paul was ready to make the trial trip, and, wearing a pair of borrowed canvas shoes, he stepped into the arena, where the ringmaster anxiously awaited his coming.

CHAPTER X.

CIRCUS LIFE IN NEW ZEALAND.

A SELECT audience had gathered in the big tent to see the property boy break his neck. On the two lower rows of reserved seats were congregated half the talent in the show, whose witticisms at Paul's expense would have quickly driven him disheartened from the field could he have heard them. But his eyes were fixed on the ringmaster and his thoughts on poor Dick, so that he barely noticed the buzz of comment which arose as he faced the manager.

"Now, my boy," began Ringmaster McIntyre, "I don't want you to have an attack of stage fright and fall off and break your neck when you get up yonder. There isn't any real danger if you don't get rattled, and I hardly think you'll do that. Are you ready to try it?"

"Yes, sir."

"Up you go, then, and good luck attend ye."

Slipping his right foot into a bowline that hung from the pole ring, and with both hands firmly clutching the rope, Paul was rapidly hauled aloft by two property boys until he reached the platform level with the wire cable where the bicycle was fastened.

Waving his hand as a signal to stop, he swung himself into the eyrie, released his foot from the loop and sent the rope down again for the use of the Kelseys.

Up they came together, laughing and chatting lightly, as if it were the jolliest picnic imaginable. Their gaiety, whether false or genuine, served to reassure Paul, who, to tell the truth, was almost in a blue funk. But he held his teeth close together to keep his heart from taking an unexpected leap outward, and a dogged determination to go through to the end possessed every fiber of his being.

Loosing the chain which pinioned the wheel to the pole, he let the machine slide along the cable until it was clear of the platform and then held it steady until the gymnasts had taken their seats on the trapeze below.

Now came his turn. For an instant he glanced below and saw the set face of the manager intently watching him from the edge of the ring. He caught a glimpse of the "main guy" on the reserved seats surrounded by the flower of the troupe, now strangely silent, and then, with a queer ringing in his ears and a slight film before his eyes, he vaulted into the saddle and was half way between the poles before he realized what had happened.

"Bravo! bravo! Chicago!" arose from a dozen throats, accompanied by a vigorous clapping of hands, as the company testified its appreciation of Paul's grit.

Arrived at the further pole, the young bicyclist reversed the action of the treadles and worked backward to the starting point, repeating the operation several times until he had acquired a perfect control of the machine.

During these preliminary trials the performers remained inactive on the bars, not deeming it prudent to attempt any of their feats until the rider had become thoroughly accustomed to the novelty of his position.

The severest test was yet to be made. After the fourth trip across, the gymnasts started in to rehearse their program, and as the wheel swayed dangerously over from left to right and then back again it was all Paul could do to keep from throwing himself from his perch and grasping the cable at his feet. But the worst shock of all came at the close, when the male tumbler, hanging suspended by his knees, caught his sister by the right wrist and left ankle, and, dexterously turning her face downward, held the girl outstretched in full view of the audience.

The suddenness of the movement carried the wheel far out to the right; then back it flew to the left of center, rocking frightfully on its grooved tires and threatening every second to become displaced. For a moment Paul had an awful feeling of nausea at the pit of his stomach, then his hair seemed to shoot straight upward, his lower limbs trembled so violently that his feet played a fandango on the treadles, and a great desire to emit an agonizing yell became paramount. But the wheel righted, the wobbling ceased, and, with the word "go" rising from below, the discomfited rider pulled himself together and slowly worked the machine back to the platform, which he quickly occupied.

Fastening the wheel to the pole, he was ready in an instant to make the descent, and a minute later was treading the sawdust and receiving the congratulations of Ringmaster McIntyre and the entire troupe. He had won his spurs and was property boy no longer.

Paul was to make his initial bow to the colonials at the matinee performance. As he could not appear in his working clothes, it was absolutely necessary that he be furnished with a suitable outfit, so the wardrobes of the entire troupe were ransacked to supply his deficiencies. A pair of slippers from one, silk tights from another, trunks from a third, a spangled vest from a fourth, with a belt and other generous contributions from the feminine side of the dressing-room, served to provide him with a handsome equipment for his new position. His trimly-built, compact figure, which showed to good advantage in his snug-fitting garments, evoked numerous comments from the performers as Paul hastened toward the big tent in response to the call from a property boy, and the sentiment was general that "Old Mac" had made a ten-strike in hiring "Chicago."

As usual, the audience filled every seat and spread over the ground clear to the edge of the ring wherein Paul and the Kelseys now stood, with the girl hand-clasped in the center, making their initiatory bows. This was no time to show the white feather, and yet that same sickening sensation which he experienced in the forenoon was insidiously stealing over him as he mounted to his aerial perch. Again he clinched his teeth, and by sheer will-force fought back the horrible feeling which threatened to overwhelm him. He wondered, as he stood there watching his companions ascend, if this were akin to stage fright, and whether it would result disastrously in spite of his efforts. His heart-beats were so violent that he fancied every person in the tent must hear them, and for a moment he held his hand at his left side as if to stifle the palpitations. But now the gymnasts were seated, there was no excuse for delay, and with a great gulp that was half sob, half sigh, he swung himself into the saddle and began anew his experiences of the morning.

All at once the unpleasant sensations left him. It was as if a leaden weight had been snatched from his shoulders and dropped into the ring below. The revulsion was so great that he could have shouted for joy had it been consistent with the dangerous part he was enacting. Back and forth he rode, utterly unmindful of the tumblings of the gymnasts, and not even at the final coup, which so upset him in the morning, did he experience the slightest tremor. There was a smile on his face that was genuine as he bowed his acknowledgments to the storm of applause which greeted the trio when they descended, and the ringmaster's cheery "Well done, Chicago," amply repaid him for the cost. But better than all was the thought that Dick's welfare was assured.

Two pounds a week in English money and his expenses was the modest stipend which MacIntyre allotted Paul for risking his neck twice a day in this manner. The sum was not large, but it more than sufficed for the lad's wants, and in a few weeks he had managed to add materially to his scanty wardrobe, which sadly needed replenishing. Before leaving Wellington he called at the hospital to see his friend Dick, but the poor fellow was delirious and failed to recognize the youngster he had befriended. His wife was pleased to see Paul, however, and warmly thanked him for his generous action, of which she had heard through her circus friends. She assured him that if Dick ever got well he would be glad to know he had not made a mistake when he played his good Samaritan act. At which Paul blushed, and, with many fervent wishes for Dick's speedy recovery, left the little circus woman dissolved in tears.

For two months following this interview Paul played his star engagement on the aerial wire without mishap and to the intense delight of thousands of good colonial subjects of Queen Victoria. In addition to the bicycle act his services were utilized in the ring to place poles for the horses to leap over; as the banner bearer, across which the bareback riders turned somersaults, and again as balloon holder, through which the lady riders dashed headlong as they careened around the circle. The boy fully earned his salary.

But he made lots of friends, too, and in a community that was always indulging in internecine quarrels, the result of petty jealousies, he retained the good-will of every one. Perhaps his warmest attachment was for the lion tamer, a stalwart, black-mustached six-footer, known as the "Parson," who, in addition to subjugating wild animals, had entire charge of the menagerie annex.

It was in the menagerie that Paul spent much of his leisure time, for he had always been partial to natural history, and this was an opportunity to study at close range not to be disregarded. "Old Tobe," the big, toothless lion, learned to know his voice, and never failed to stick out his paw for a friendly shake when the lad passed his cage. Tiny "Mimi," a pretty little marmoset monkey, would chatter with delight when Paul approached her, and at his departure would cling to the bars and cry piteously for his return. Even vicious "Potiphar," the black elephant that had killed two of his keepers, permitted Paul to fondle his trunk and feed him crackers, a supply of which he usually kept in his pocket when he visited the elephants.

There was one member of the "Parson's" family with which Paul could never get on intimate terms, despite all his friendly advances. This was a beautifully spotted tigress called Satan, which the lion tamer had formerly exhibited when she was younger, but whose ugly temper had compelled him to desert after two or three attempts that nearly cost him his life.

One day, while showing at a place called Timaru, along ninety-mile beach in the middle island, Satan broke loose from her cage. The time she chose for this pleasantry was immediately following the afternoon performance, when, luckily, the menagerie was pretty well deserted, only Paul and the attendants chancing to be present. Feeding time had arrived, and a mass of raw meat, placed inadvertently in front of her cage, had so tantalized Satan that she tore up the floor near the front of her prison, and, squeezing through, with a wild scream of delight reached in a bound the quivering meat for which she hungered.

At that moment Paul was feeding tiny "Mimi," the pet monkey, not a dozen steps from where Satan lay crouching and snarling. The shouts of terror from the scattering attendants and the hasty glance he caught of the liberated animal were enough to cause him to join the others in a mad rush for safety, and in a minute he was shinning up the main guy of the center pole as if a battalion of wildcats was hot on his trail.

The "Parson" was feeding his pet lions strips of raw beef when Satan's triumphant cries rang through the menagerie, and although his back was toward the tigress he divined instantly what had happened. Seizing his heavily loaded whip, without a moment's hesitation, the intrepid fellow strode across to where Satan lay worrying a bloody bone. She growled savagely as he approached, and began lashing her beautiful tail from right to left, while her long, supple spine gradually arched as she rose for a spring.

From his coign of vantage aloft Paul was an intensely interested spectator of what followed. He saw the lion-tamer concentrate his fearless gaze on the escaped brute, which for one moment quailed before his piercing eyes. That moment was fatal to her hopes of liberty. Like a flash of lightning the loaded whip leaped in the air and descended with the force of a sledge hammer on Satan's skull. She sunk back with a long wailing cry of distress that was almost human, and in two minutes lay insensible under the terrific blows administered by her trainer.

By this time half a dozen attendants had rushed to the rescue, when, with a single sarcastic reference to their tardiness, their chief curtly ordered the animal placed in stronger quarters and placidly returned to the task from which he had been so abruptly summoned.

The lion tamer chuckled as he caught sight of Paul's lithe figure slipping down the center pole, and he was still smiling when the lad joined him in front of the hyenas' cage, which happened to be next that in which the attendants were depositing Satan.

"Say, son, you made pretty good time getting up there, didn't you?" he observed, in his quiet, drawling tones.

Paul blushed and looked sheepish, but before he could answer, the sturdy trainer remarked: "Oh, well, I don't blame you for it, boy; but I might have expected something different from my own men." And that was the only rebuke the big-hearted giant launched toward his weak-kneed attendants, nor did he ever recur to the subject.

By gradual stages the circus covered all the principal towns of the middle island, and at length reached the pretty city of Christchurch, in the province

of Canterbury, where a two weeks' stand was on the program. At this place the troupe was reinforced by the arrival of Dick Baxter and his wife, the former still too weak to work, but entirely recovered from his illness and rapidly growing stronger.

He greeted Paul very kindly, thanked him cordially for what he had done, but insisted on turning over half his salary to his substitute. To this the latter stoutly demurred, and ended by flatly refusing the proffered money. Finding him obdurate, Dick sought a jeweler's and purchased a plain, broad band of Australian gold, inside which he had engraved:

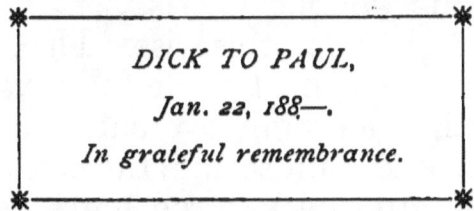

DICK TO PAUL,

Jan. 22, 188—.

In grateful remembrance.

Paul wore this ring in sickness and starvation, in trouble and danger, all through that eventful trip until he was safe home again. And he wears it to this day, although the donor has long since lain at rest beneath the tropic skies of South America, a victim of a broken cable and his own temerity.

It was the last day of Paul's appearance in tights and spangles, for Dick was to resume his duties on the morrow. Sitting on a bale of hay out in the menagerie tent, the lad was cogitating upon his next move. To return to the drudgery of "Old Props'" rule was too distasteful after the glitter and glare of the ring, and the offer of peddling popcorn, peanuts and the clown's song books was not at all to his fancy. Circus life, in fact, was beginning to pall on him, when an incident occurred which thoroughly settled the question in his mind and left no hesitating doubts.

It happened in this wise: The "boss hostler," a man of powerful physique, but with a most ungovernable temper, had accused Paul several times of carrying cigarettes over to the horse tent to give to one of the hostlers, a half-breed Maori, to whom the lad had taken a great fancy. This was true, but when "Texas," as the boss hostler was nicknamed, swore the boy smoked them around the hay and abetted the Maori in breaking the rules, the youngster hotly resented the charge, and called on the half-breed to prove that he never smoked either in or out of the tent.

"Oh, he's just as big a liar as you are," snarled Texas.

"You wouldn't say that twice if I were a man," retorted Paul savagely.

"Bah! You're a kid, and the nigger's a fool. After this just keep out of my quarters, or it'll be the worse for you," and the surly brute strode off.

Furious, but powerless, Paul turned to "Pete," the half-breed, whose coal-black eyes shone with suppressed rage.

"I kill that devil some day," he hissed, "if he no let me be; I hate him."

Soothing the Maori with a few well-chosen words, the boy quitted the tent and returned to the dressing room to get ready for the evening performance—his last appearance.

Two hours later, his act over, he heard Texas blackguarding his hostlers for some fancied slight in adjusting the pads on the riding horses, and just as he was slipping into his street clothes another wave of profanity floated across the intervening space, the intensity of which proved that Texas was in a towering passion.

Fearful that the Maori was getting into trouble, and with a vague notion of averting some possible calamity, Paul hastily drew on his coat, wrapped a piece of spare canvas about his head and shoulders as a partial protection from the pouring rain, and darted outside the dressing room across to the horse tent.

He arrived just in time to see Texas pick up an empty bucket and bring it down with all his might on Pete's head. The wicked blow shattered the pail but did not break the Maori's skull. Howling with rage and pain the half-breed seized a heavy, iron-bound stakepin that lay at his feet and before anyone could divine his intentions or stay his hand the murderous billet descended with terrific force on the circus man's right temple, and Texas dropped like a log. Not contented with this the Maori repeated the blows again and again, and before assistance arrived the position of boss hostler in the great American consolidated arenas stood temporarily vacant.

Without an instant's delay the crazed half-breed jumped across the body of his victim, darted into a vacant stall, lifted the flap of the tent, and disappeared in the black, pelting storm.

But Paul had no heart for the circus after that. He had been an accidental witness of the fearful tragedy, powerless to prevent it, too horrified to speak or move a step, and yet he accused himself of participating in the crime because he had lacked presence of mind to cry out to the Maori to desist. He did not realize, poor lad, that it was a demon, not a human, which possessed the half-breed in those brief moments, and that he might just as well have tried to stop the howling of the north wind. For two days longer he stayed with the troupe, and then went to the red wagon, drew what little salary was due him, bade goodbye to his friends and left the circus forever.

CHAPTER XI.

ON SHIPBOARD AGAIN.

The city of Christchurch is seven miles inland from the port of Lyttleton, and for a good part of that distance a railroad is tunnelled through solid rock, an engineering feat of which the Canterbury provincials have good reason to be proud. It was a gloomy journey for Paul, whose spirits were not of the brightest, but a sniff of the fresh, salt sea after his stuffy ride had a cheering effect, and he soon forgot his troubles in the effort to get a berth.

It was his intention to ship from Lyttleton aboard one of the passenger steamers plying between New Zealand and Australian ports—Melbourne preferred—which city he was eager to visit. But he was not more fortunate in obtaining a billet here than at San Francisco, and after meeting a dozen rebuffs he gave up the attempt and secured passage on a small coaster to

Dunedin, one of the principal cities of New Zealand.

At Dunedin, a bustling, busy city of fifty thousand inhabitants, settled mainly by the thrifty Scotch, Paul stayed three weeks, vainly endeavoring to secure a position in any capacity on one of the many steamers touching at that port. His small savings, although carefully handled, slowly melted away during this period of idleness, and by the end of the third week he had dispensed with one or two articles of his wardrobe which he began to regard as unnecessary luxuries.

The outlook was blue, and the boy several times thought regretfully of the circus and his three meals a day, and wondered if he hadn't been too hasty in burning his ships. One bright afternoon, while sitting on a mooring block at the wharf, watching the steamer for Melbourne and Sydney make fast, and mentally wishing he were aboard her, he spied a familiar figure trot across the gangway that had just been lowered from the vessel's side. In a minute he was off his perch, yelling, "Davy, O Davy!" at the top of his voice.

The cause of this sudden outburst was a slim lad about Paul's own age, who, hearing his name called, halted irresolutely, until, tracing the sound, he gave a shout of recognition and came up the dock on a run.

"Hello, Paul!" he exclaimed. "What in the world are you doing here? Thought you was with the circus!"

"So I was up to a month ago, when I tired of the job and quit. But say, what are you doing on the Koturah?"

"Working, faith. Shipped as brass trimmer and lamp cleaner at Auckland trip before this and like the billet first rate. 'Nough sight better than the hotel, I can tell you."

Davy Marston had been a sort of boy-of-all-work at the hotel in Auckland where Paul and the circus hands boarded while the show was in that city and the two lads had become quite intimate. Davy was a slender, dreamy kind of a chap, whose parents were both dead, so that he had been compelled to shift for himself at an early age. Bright, cheerful and obliging, he was a most companionable little fellow, toward whom Paul had been greatly attracted. When the troupe left town Davy caught the fever for travel and decided to go away, too, and through the good offices of the local agent of the steamship company he obtained a berth on the Koturah, with which ship he had made the round trip to Australia and was now on his second voyage. He declared money couldn't hire him to work on shore again.

Paul sighed. "Wish I could strike a piece of luck like that," he dolefully exclaimed. "Do you suppose there's any show for me on board, Davy?"

The boy puckered his forehead and thought a minute. "Seems to me I heard the pantryman say they were shorthanded in the galley. Tell you what I'll do: Wait here while I skip back and see if I can't put in a few good licks for you. Don't count on me too much, but I'll do the very best I can."

Away sped the good-hearted young colonial, leaving Paul intently praying for the success of his mission. In twenty minutes the lad returned, his honest face wreathed in smiles.

"Did it up brown," he gasped, between breaths. "You're to get your kit and come aboard right away. Cook says he'll find a place for you in the galley helping him."

Barely stopping to express his gratitude, off Paul started for his boarding house, where he settled his bill with the last shilling he possessed, hastily threw his belongings in his valise and rushed back to the vessel, where Davy was on hand waiting to receive him.

Half an hour later Paul might have been seen in the ship's galley, seated on an inverted bucket, his coat off, and his sleeves rolled back to his elbows, peeling "spuds" as if he had served a life apprenticeship at the task. And Davy chancing by the open doorway chuckled audibly at the sight, a significant wink from Paul helping him to a keener appreciation of the joke.

The days which ensued were full of interest to the young Chicagoan, who was too happy planning for the future to feel at all humiliated by the drudgery of his work. Leaving Port Chalmers behind, the Koturah's next stop was at the Bluff, and then the boat headed direct for Melbourne, reaching Port Philip after a delightful run. It had been Paul's idea all along to quit the vessel at Melbourne, to which point he intended having his mail forwarded from Sydney, but his relations on board had been so pleasant that when Davy urged him to go on as far as Sydney he was easily persuaded.

Before Port Jackson Heads were sighted one of the understewards was taken seriously ill, and when the Koturah steamed alongside her dock at the circular quay his condition was so alarming that the ship's doctor advised his removal to the city hospital, where he could have better care. This made a vacancy on the saloon staff, which the chief steward was disposed to fill by offering Paul the position.

The temptation to stay a while longer in such pleasant quarters was so strong that after a short mental struggle Paul yielded and gracefully accepted the proffered advancement. But before the boat cast loose on her return trip to Auckland he obtained leave to go up town to inquire for his mail, a goodly budget of which he fully expected to find awaiting him at the postoffice.

Nor was he disappointed. Big, fat letters in the dear, well-known handwriting were given him bearing the old, familiar Chicago postmark, half blurred, it is true, as usual, but still decipherable. He strolled over into Cook Park for an undisturbed reading, and, sitting on a bench near the colossal statue of the great circumnavigator in whose honor the park is named, greedily devoured the thrice welcome epistles.

Letters from home. Only those who have journeyed thousands of miles from all they hold dear, and who have been deprived of all news regarding them for endless weeks, can appreciate with what trembling anxiety Paul tore open his first letter. He laughed and cried by turns as he read the closely written pages from his mother which told of Madge's clever sayings, of Edith's longings for her comrade brother, of his father's latest fit of ludicrous forgetfulness and of the hundred and one petty details of home life, every item of which was of intensest interest to the wanderer.

Now that her boy was fairly launched on his long tramp, the gentle mother had ceased grieving on account of his absence, but on every page her messages of caution predominated. As Paul absorbed the loving admonitions his eyes became blurred and the tears stole swiftly down his cheeks, to be stemmed a moment later as he read some particularly bright bit of absurdity credited to his light-hearted, mirth-loving sister, Madge. All the letters were penned in a cheerful spirit, as if the writers were determined to leave the recipient in a pleasant frame of mind following their perusal. After an hour spent in reading and re-reading the precious missives the lad stowed them carefully away in an inside pocket and strolled back to the ship, pensive but happy.

Paul had heard much about the beauties of Sydney harbor since his advent in southern waters, but the realization of them far exceeded his expectations. As the stately Koturah steamed down the bay on her way to Port Jackson Heads, in the full glare of the noonday sun, a panorama of entrancing loveliness was unfolded that held the lad spellbound. All this he had missed on the up-trip, owing to the lateness of the hour in entering the harbor, so that he now for the first time saw the bay in all its matchless splendor.

The waters were dotted with big and little craft of every description. The gently sloping banks on either side were crowned with luxuriant foliage, amid which the eye caught glimpses of charming white villas with wide, cool-looking verandas and green-jalousied blinds, which lent a semi-tropical and wholly delightful aspect to the harmonious picture. That its natural beauties and excellent anchorage entitled the bay of Sydney to be accounted one of the finest harbors in the world Paul did not question, and he reluctantly turned away from the enchanting vision to answer a peremptory call from below, where his services were needed.

Outside Port Jackson Heads, into the Pacific ocean, the Koturah plowed her way with the fairest weather abreast her keel that heart could desire. It was not surprising that, stirred by the sight of the broad, silvery moon, the pondlike stillness of the water, and the soft, balmy breezes sighing through the shrouds, the younger people on board should be eager to take advantage of a situation so delightful. The consent of the captain being gained, a deck concert and dance was planned, the proceeds arising from which it was proposed to donate to the Shipwrecked Mariners' Society of New South Wales.

As everybody was expected to contribute in some way to the success of the entertainment, the understewards were on their mettle. One was a good banjo-player, another a capital mimic, and a third was clever at sleight-of-hand tricks. Paul was urged by his new comrades to give a Yankee recitation, and readily agreed to do his share. The second night out from

Sydney Captain Barrett had the after-deck canopied with flags and bunting, the piano was brought up from the saloon, benches were improvised for the audience, and the passengers responded gallantly to the invitation to fill the seats. Interspersed among them were the sailors, arrayed in their best outfits, their blue jerseys and white hats producing a very pleasing effect in the soft light shed by the Chinese lanterns.

Overhead shone the brilliant Southern Cross, the sharp outlines of which could be traced through the thin fabric of the Union Jacks which formed a partial protection from the night dews. The water was like glass; a generous moon trailed her silvery sheen in the vessel's wake, and as the musical notes of the sweet soprano soloist drifted away from the ship it required no great stretch of imagination to believe that every tiny wavelet rippling in the molten beams was the head of a mermaid enticed to the surface by the wonderful charms of the human voice.

Vocal and instrumental music in solos, duets and quartets followed in delightful succession, alternating with readings and recitations by the combined ship's talent. Paul's modest rendition of Will Carleton's "Betsy and I Are Out," with its homely pathos, seemed to strike a popular chord in the breasts of the audience, and the "young Yankee" was vigorously applauded, an encore being demanded. He responded with John Hay's "Little Breeches," the delivery of which completely captured the colonists and evoked a lot of pleasant compliments that were not entirely undeserved.

The concert ended, the benches were carried away, the deck was cleared for action, and with piano and fiddle for music, the younger passengers enjoyed the novelty of a dance in mid-ocean. Promptly at midnight the captain gave the signal for "Home, Sweet Home," the tune changing quickly to "God Save the Queen," which brought all the loyal colonials to their feet, and closed the evening's unique entertainment.

At Auckland the Koturah landed the majority of her Australian passengers, but a new batch was shipped in their stead. At Wellington and Lyttleton their numbers were greatly augmented by a delegation of ministers and their families who were on their way to South Australia to attend an annual conference, so that by the time Dunedin was reached every inch of cabin space on the ship was taken.

The Koturah was not one of the best boats in the service, but she was a good, stout vessel, and, having been recently overhauled and thoroughly repaired, was considered perfectly safe. Her skipper, Captain Barrett, although a young man, was extremely popular, as much on account of his amiable disposition as for his excellent seamanship, so that the Koturah usually carried a fine passenger list.

On this occasion she was taxed to her capacity, due to the fact that, instead of proceeding direct to Melbourne from the Bluff, she was advertised to go first to Adelaide, in order to accommodate the number of people desirous of attending conference in the South Australian colony. The beautiful weather which had prevailed so long attracted a much larger number of excursionists than was expected, and when the boat left Dunedin she had seventy people in the first and second cabins and about eighty steerage passengers.

Naturally the work of attending to the wants of so many people gave Paul very few leisure moments, so that he and Davy had little time to visit or gossip. Late in the evening, after leaving Dunedin, the two boys met in the steward's room for a short chat, when Paul was dismayed to find his chum looking unusually serious and depressed.

"Why, what ails you to-night, Davy?" he asked. "You're as glum as a hired mourner."

"I know it, Paul, and the worst of it is I can't get over the feeling. It's all on account of a dream I had last night. I thought I was lying on the bottom of the ocean with my eyes wide open, watching a procession of drowned persons dropping down, down, down, from the surface, directly before me, and each face bore such a sorrowful expression that I was terrified, and I know that I must have cried out in my sleep. The picture was so vivid that I couldn't forget it when I woke up, and do you know, Paul," here the lad lowered his voice to a whisper, "I have been seeing those same faces all day and they've taken on the features of our new passengers. It scares me; I feel as if something awful was going to happen, and I can't get rid of the notion to save my life. You may laugh, perhaps, and say it's all nonsense—maybe it is—but the thing sticks. Ugh! it's a horrible sensation," and the boy shuddered.

Paul didn't laugh. Davy had told his dream so simply, yet so earnestly, that he felt impressed in spite of his inclination to look upon the whole matter as an ordinary nightmare arising from overwork and a nervous physical condition. He saw Davy was greatly disturbed, so wisely refrained from treating the story too lightly. "Oh, well, old fellow," he exclaimed, in his cheeriest tones, "I wouldn't fret about it; you know that won't do any good. If I were you I'd turn in right away and get a good sleep. You'll feel better in the morning."

Davy slowly shook his head, and, placing his hand over his heart, brokenly observed: "It's here I feel it. There's such a leaden weight that it seems as if something must give way. Say, do you believe in omens?" he abruptly inquired.

Paul hesitated before answering. "I don't know; I have read of some very queer manifestations," he presently admitted, "but I never had any personal experiences. Why?"

"Because," said Davy, very solemnly and impressively, "I am certain that dream of mine is coming true. Something tells me I shall never get off this boat alive. I can't describe my sensations; nothing like the feeling ever took hold of me before, but I believe I am—am doomed," and, dropping his face between his hands, the sensitive, overwrought boy burst into a paroxysm of tears.

His companion was greatly shocked and more powerfully moved than he cared to admit even to himself. "Oh, come, come, Davy, you mustn't go on like this or you'll be ill. Let me go to the doctor and get a prescription to quiet your nerves and put you to sleep. You've been working too hard, that's what's the trouble. Brace up, old fellow, and don't get frightened by a mere dream. You'll have forgotten it by this time to-morrow."

He passed his arm caressingly around the neck of the perturbed boy and patted his shoulder as he strove to soothe and reassure him. Presently the sobs ceased and Davy raised his tear-swollen face. "You're a good chap, Paul," he said, with an effort to keep his voice steady, "and I'm so glad that I was able to do you a service. I want you to think well of me, no matter what happens. Perhaps I'm a bit foolish after all." Then he wrung his friend's hand, choked back a sob and turned away. And after he was gone Paul remembered with a queer thrill that it was "good-bye" and not "goodnight" that Davy had said.

The recollection troubled him. He was altogether too sturdy and healthy a lad to be in the least superstitious, but as he strolled meditatively toward his bunk that "good-bye" rung in his ears until he was almost tempted to follow Davy to his berth and ask him what it meant. But this, he concluded, might lead to another painful scene, so, shrugging his shoulders as if to throw off an unpleasant load, he decided to turn in for the night.

Half a dozen of the under-stewards sat around the sleeping quarters in various stages of undress as Paul entered the compartment. Some of them had been discussing the ship's course, and one of the older boys remarked that the meanest part of the trip was just ahead. He explained that the passage from Dunedin to the bluff, which, as they well knew, is the southernmost point on the island, was considered very dangerous on account of the extremely rocky coast and because the course in some parts lies right between ugly reefs on one side and a number of half-submerged rocks shoreward. Added to this was a treacherous swell, requiring smart navigation to take a vessel through safely, particularly in muggy weather.

"Of course," he oracularly added,

"there's no danger when a man like Capt. Barrett's on watch, and the old Koturah's been through too often to get caught napping; but, just the same, I'd as lief be round the point and headed for Adelaide." With which comforting observation he kicked off his shoes and disappeared in his bunk.

It was a long time before Paul slept. The vision of Davy's sorrowful face haunted him, and then, too, the yarn spun by the under-steward, now blissfully snoring, aroused a vague feeling of uneasiness which would not be suppressed. Eight bells, midnight, struck before he finally lost consciousness. His last waking thoughts were centered in a strange fancy regarding Davy and his dead parents. He found himself wondering if they had been the cause of his chum's grewsome dream, and whether, after all, it was not a note of warning from the other world.

CHAPTER XII.

WRECK OF THE KOTURAH.

HE awoke suddenly, a frightened yell from one of the boys causing him to spring from his bunk into the middle of the room. As he did so a horrible, grinding sound was heard, which seemed to come from the heart of the boat and was accompanied by a series of shocks that racked the vessel from stem to stern. This was followed by a succession of bumps which threatened to pound the timbers into kindling wood.

With a sickening intuition of some great disaster, Paul scrambled into his clothes, disregarding the babel of helpless questions hurled at each other by the panic-stricken stewards. Pulling his cap on tight and buttoning his coat as he ran along the passage, the lad mounted the companionway two steps at a jump, and in less than a minute reached the deck above.

It was about 5 o'clock in the morning. The stars still appeared overhead, but a heavy mist enveloped the entire ship, rendering it impossible to see twenty feet in any direction. There was no need to ask foolish questions. It was only too evident, from the repeated concussions, that the vessel had struck a reef, and like a flash the gossip of the night previous and, above all, poor Davy's dream darted across Paul's brain. He peered anxiously about for a sight of his chum, but in that uncertain light, and with a score or more of hysterical passengers running helplessly in every direction, the search was useless, and he turned his attention to the half-dressed women and children who crowded up from below, weeping and wringing their hands.

The spectacle presented by the helpless, frightened women and terrified children was one long to be remembered. Their shrieks and cries of despair served to intensify the awful situation, and lent additional horror to the scene. The bumping continued incessantly, and the ship very soon began to fill with water which poured in through a big gash in her stern quarter. The Koturah was fast between two jagged, gaping rocks, which she had struck almost head on. Although the engines had been stopped and reversed, it was too late to be of any service. Apparently the boat was doomed.

It was impossible to make any movement looking to a rescue until the fog lifted or daylight broke, and his utter helplessness for the moment unnerved the captain, who met the piteous appeals of the passengers with equally depressing responses. Then, seeing the bad effect this temporary weakness produced, by a supreme effort the skipper pulled himself together and in a voice that was surprisingly steady issued orders for every passenger to form in a circle around the mainmast until he and his officers should decide what was best to be done.

In half an hour the mist cleared a bit and as daylight waxed stronger the seriousness of the situation was revealed. The boat was ashore on a very dangerous reef at the most desolate, inhospitable point along the entire New Zealand coast. The swell was so terrific that every few minutes huge seas broke over the vessel, carrying off all loose fixtures in their resistless rush and such of the unfortunate passengers who chanced to be caught in their mighty embrace.

After a hurried consultation it was decided that communication with land must be essayed immediately, and Captain Barrett ordered one of the forward boats to be cleared for lowering. As it swung ready over the side a score of steerage passengers crowded up with the intention of forcing their way in, but the determined manner in which the commander wielded a stout belaying pin had the effect of quelling their ardor. Scowling and muttering they fell back, sulky but subdued.

The boat was lowered away, but the moment it struck the water it was lifted clean off the tackle by which it was suspended and dashed against the ship's side, filling and sinking at once. The pilot boat was then made ready and swung over at a point where the water was a little smoother. This attempt was successful and the passengers cheered when the second officer, Mr. Riley, with six sailors and a volunteer from the steerage, climbed in and pulled away.

In about an hour Riley returned and reported that on account of the heavy surf it was impossible to get within 500 feet of the shore, but the passenger, a young fellow named Carey from Timaru, had jumped overboard and swum safely to land, as he was afterward seen climbing a bluff and waving his hands.

The captain looked glum when he received this bit of news. He had fully expected to be able to land his passengers with the aid of the boats, but it was evident from Riley's statement that the women and children stood a poor chance of escape in that direction. Even a good swimmer was likely to be drowned in the treacherous surf. Another hasty conference followed, and then it was decided to try to pass a line ashore from the ship, that appearing to be the only possible method of effecting a landing.

Riley and his men being pretty

well exhausted, the captain called for volunteers—those only who could swim—and six of the steerage passengers pressing forward, he placed the boat in charge of the first mate, with instructions to use every endeavor to get a line to the shore.

It looked then as if the vessel were the safer place, which probably accounted for the few who offered to leave. As soon as the volunteer crew was off Captain Barrett ordered the women and children moved forward to the smoking room, amidships, where there was more protection from the seas, which now began to make frightful sweeps over the afterpart of the vessel.

It was during one of these mighty washes that poor Davy was carried away. The lad had been sent below to fish out a lantern, and just as his head appeared above deck a loose spar struck him and keeled him over. He staggered to his feet, but at that moment a terrific volume of water was impelled over the vessel's side, and as it rushed away to port poor Davy was whirled along with it as if he had been a cork. Paul caught one glimpse of his white, despairing face as he rose for an instant on the crest of the waves, and then the boy was swept out of sight forever.

Shocking as the accident was, Paul had not a moment to spend in shedding tears for his lost chum, although his heart was like lead. The living miseries all around him forbade yielding to any weakness, no matter how great the provocation. There were women weeping and children sobbing; women that were half-dressed, with wild eyes and disheveled hair, who held their little ones close to their breasts and alternately wept and prayed in their hysterical anguish. To them he gave his constant attention, now soothing a frightened child and presently uttering words of cheer to a distracted mother. The lad entirely forgot his own discomforts and peril and for hours devoted himself to alleviating in some measure the misfortunes of the poor creatures, who appeared to have lost all self-control in the presence of this awful catastrophe.

It was not that Paul was any braver

than the rest, but his spirits seemed to become more buoyant in the face of danger, and a strong determination to contest to the end took irresistible possession of him. He could not believe that he was doomed to drown after so many escapes elsewhere on that momentous journey, and the thought gave him additional courage. There was no philosophy in this, perhaps, but the idea was comforting, and the lad cherished it accordingly.

Chancing to be near the captain, shortly after the first officer left with his volunteer crew, Paul was attracted by the earnest manner in which the skipper followed with his glass the receding boat. Presently he saw him make a gesture of despair and with an agonized face turn to the second engineer.

"Mack! Mack!" he exclaimed, "this is awful. The boat's swamped and Pearson and his men are in the breakers. A blind roller knocked 'em endways and I'm afraid everyone is drowned. For heaven's sake keep quiet about it; the passengers are scared enough already. I must send Riley out again to make another trial."

The second mate, with three sailors and three volunteers, manned a second boat and succeeded in getting clear of the reef. Only the mate knew of the disaster which had overtaken the first officer. There was no need to caution him about keeping a sharp lookout, for he realized that the fate of the entire ship depended largely on the success of his efforts.

It was 10 o'clock before the second boat was launched, and the four hours of daylight had given everyone an opportunity to form some idea of the desperate situation in which the ship was placed. The Koturah was apparently a hopeless wreck, with her nose jammed hard and fast on the ugliest reef to be found anywhere along the New Zealand coast. A big hole in her stern quarter admitted tons of water at each wash of the seas, every influx of which materially weakened the structure. Groaning and writhing as if in mortal agony from the strain, the vessel threatened to go to pieces at any moment. So long as her bows remained nipped in the jaws of the reef she was fairly safe, but the constant shocks make this a very uncertain tenure. Captain Barrett was right in believing it an imperative necessity to either effect a landing on the coast or take the remaining boats and pull out to sea. Why he did not adopt the latter course while the opportunity lasted will never be known.

Paul was not the only person who wondered why the ship chanced to be so near shore when she struck. From a hasty explanation he overheard Captain Barrett giving the chief engineer he learned that on account of the heavy fog the skipper had mistaken his position, and, not making due allowance for the southerly swell, imagined the Koturah lay much farther out. When the ship struck the second mate was in charge of the deck, the captain having just retired, believing all was well. The boat was running about ten knots an hour—a good average speed. The lookout, thinking he heard the breakers, reported to the mate, who ran to call the captain instead of acting instantly himself. The delay proved fatal. Hurrying on deck, Captain Barrett scented the danger immediately and ordered the helm hard-a-starboard and the engines reversed, but the headway was so great that before she could swing around the vessel went on the rocks.

For two long hours the half-drowned passengers watched and waited for Riley's return. Cold, hungry, and wet to the skin, a more miserable set of human beings could scarcely have been found. At 12 o'clock the captain instructed the chief steward to try to pass some kind of food forward for the passengers and crew, few of whom had eaten a mouthful since the night previous. For this service two volunteers were called. The pantryman, a bright young fellow from Geelong, and Paul were the first to respond, and a line being made fast to the waist of each the two clasped hands and watched their opportunity to dash aft to the storeroom.

Almost drowned in the attempt, they managed to emerge with a supply of soaked crackers, some tinned meats and an Edam cheese which they had hastily thrown into a canvas bag that was fastened to the pantryman's belt. There was not enough to go around, so it was divided among the shivering women and hungry, crying children. A second venture was essayed and the bag filled with hard biscuit, which sorry food was apportioned among the male passengers and crew.

Probably few on the Koturah at that time fully realized their imminent peril. The fog having completely lifted, land was seen comparatively close by and occasionally the dim outlines of persons moving about on the shore could be discerned. It was not until Riley's absence became so prolonged that hope began to pale, for, the tide coming in, the sea grew much rougher and poured continuously through the ship, which was likely to go to pieces at any minute.

During a temporary lull the second mate was seen trying to make up to the vessel, but on account of the heavy swell he found it impossible to get alongside. After repeated efforts he was forced to desist, and with a despairing gesture he waved a good-by and pulled out to the open sea, where the waves were calmer and the chances of being dashed on the reef more remote.

This action on the part of his subordinate decided Captain Barrett to waste no more precious time in trying to effect a landing on the cruel coast. But before he could put his plan into execution a perfect avalanche of water descended on the doomed ship, carrying away the long boat, cutter and dingy, and leaving him entirely helpless. As if in furious competition for their prey this was followed by another monstrous wave, which swooped down upon the helpless wreck from the opposite quarter, tearing away a big section of the forward bulwarks, behind which nearly a score of passengers were crouched. In a moment all were precipitated in the angry waters, their piteous appeals for help falling on the ears of those who were powerless to render the slightest assistance.

This fearful disaster, which might be their own fate any moment, had a most depressing effect on the survivors, who were now collected in the fo'castle, which was, perhaps, the least exposed part of the ship. About twenty persons were left out of 200 souls. Some of the women were clad only in their underclothing and night dresses, over which a ship's blanket had been hastily thrown. All were soaked through with salt water and suffered acutely from cold and hunger, physical discomforts which, however, were not to be compared with the mental tortures they endured.

As the afternoon waned and the dreaded night wore on the situation grew more agonizing. At about 7 o'clock one of the sailors, lashed to the foremast, shouted: "Lights! Lights! A boat in sight." Paul glanced at the captain, but he shook his head despairingly; no vessel could possibly approach near enough the treacherous rocks to be of service. And so it proved. After trying in vain to beat up toward them, she was at length compelled for her own safety to bear out to sea.

Since the loss of the small boats the only hope of rescue lay in assistance from a passing vessel, and when the passengers saw the ship's lights growing dimmer and less distinct some of them lost all control and fell to cursing and praying alternately, while the heartrending shrieks of agonized women and the repressed sobbing of their more self-contained sisters added to the frightful picture of desolation. One old, white-haired minister from Napier tried to sing "Rock of Ages," but his voice trembled so that he broke down completely and ended by blending his tears with those of the unfortunate females.

During all this long, miserable day, by his many little acts of unselfishness and his devotion to the weak, trembling women, whom he tried in every way known to a courageous heart to comfort and cheer, Paul had greatly endeared himself to the captain, and the latter several times thanked the quiet-spoken American lad for his thoughtful and timely services.

As they crouched together in the fo'castle, waiting for the vessel's dissolution and what seemed to be certain death, Captain Barrett suddenly bent down to Paul, who was supporting the limp figure of a little girl, whose parents had been swept away.

"Travers," he hoarsely whispered.

"Yes, sir."

"If by any chance you get to shore alive I want you to see the owners and tell them that if I made a mistake I did what I believed was for the best. Will you do this for me?"

"Gladly, sir, if I get the chance."

"That's all, Travers. You've been a great help to me, a great comfort, lad, and may—may God bless and preserve you." Then he wrung the boy's hand in token of farewell, stifled a groan that was half a sob and turned to speak a word of cheer to the second engineer, who, with a crushed leg, was propped up against the foremast.

Poor Paul's sympathy for the broken-hearted commander caused his tears to flow unchecked on the damp locks of his little charge, who had cried herself to sleep on his breast. Growing calmer he breathed an inward prayer for his own deliverance and fervently entreated the Almighty that the brave captain might be included among the saved.

From 8 o'clock until midnight the only change in the tense situation was a last move of the survivors from the fo'castle to the rigging, made necessary as the wreck settled lower and lower in the water. It was not accomplished without incredible exertions, due to the limp and exhausted condition of the women, who were more than half dead from fright and the terrible exposure. By supporting the maimed engineer between them Paul and the captain helped the brave fellow to a position beyond the reach of the waves, although he begged them to leave him to his fate. It was just prior to this change of base that the good old minister pronounced a touching prayer invoking the blessing of the Almighty upon those who were now apparently beyond all earthly assistance.

To Paul, young, vigorous and with the love of life strong within him, these last hours in the rigging were peculiarly trying ones. Isolated for the first time that day, each one lashed in place to prevent a surprise by the angry waves, he was left to his own thoughts, which were anything but inspiring. To come so far in safety and then to die like this! It seemed too cruel, too unreal! He could not believe it possible and his soul in anguish rebelled against his impending fate. He closed his eyes tight to shut out the horrible, ghostly figures, lashed all around him, and his thoughts flew to that far-away home on the shores of Lake Michigan. Before his mental vision rose those dear faces, now, perhaps, lost to him forever! It could not, must not be! He would fight for his life to the last! If all else were drowned he must be saved! He was too young too die! There was so much that he had planned to do! Surely he was not to be cut off so soon. And then there was his mother! "Ah, God!" he prayed, "let me live to see my dear mother once more!"

A despairing cry from one of the unfortunate creatures near him recalled Paul to the awful scenes in which he was a participant. He opened his eyes in time to see a young woman—she was a bride of two days when she left Wellington, but her husband had been drowned early in the day—drop from her fastenings, and, striking the lower shrouds, rebound thence into the dark waters. The boy was past weeping; a lump rose in his throat as he thought of the poor girl and the sweet picture she made when, leaning on her husband's arm, she proudly tripped across the gangway at Wellington. But there were no tears to shed; he was beyond that. He could only groan as he felt his heartstrings vibrate, and he dumbly wondered if they would snap under the strain.

Then he turned his eyes shoreward, where the sparse watchers had built huge bonfires, whose bright flames could be plainly seen from the rigging. Occasionally a weird figure might be discerned flitting across the beach or piling more wood on the blaze. That the wreck was visible to those on land Paul did not doubt, for the glare from the fires flashed across the ship whenever fresh fuel was added.

But it would have been madness to venture out; a boat had no chance for existence in the heavy seas that were running, even if it escaped the treacherous surf. Then, too, there were the rocks, those gaping, jagged reefs on which the Koturah had received her mortal wound. No, there was nothing to do but to wait for death or the morning. If the ship held together until daylight there was still a hope for rescue in case the seas went down. But the chances were slim. The boat was settling fast, and as the waves mounted higher and still higher toward the wretched survivors the weaker ones gradually lost all power of resistance, and parting their lashings dropped into the watery grave which greedily engulfed them.

CHAPTER XIII.

IN GOOD SAMARITANS' HANDS.

ANOTHER painful hour passed, during which scarcely a word was spoken by the few miserable beings that remained alive. The wreck, meantime, had been gradually settling until the deck was entirely under water and the waves repeatedly dashed over the helpless creatures in the rigging. Suddenly the boat gave a frightful lurch which lowered her fully five feet and told the half dozen forlorn souls hanging on for their lives that the end was very near.

Paul knew it was now only a question of minutes when the entire ship would be submerged. Slipping his lashings and tightening the cork belt which was fastened under his armpits, he began to prepare for the final struggle. He realized there was little hope in such a sea and among those death-dealing rocks, but he was not going to give up without a determined fight for his life.

Just as he was about to climb still higher to avoid the drenching seas an immense wave struck him with terrific force, loosening his grip and knocking him clean off his perch into the foaming billows. Down, down he went, meantime holding his breath and striving hard to retain his senses. When at length he rose to the surface he kicked out vigorously, but had not taken a dozen strokes when his head bumped against a hard substance, and for a moment the boy thought he was on the dreaded rocks.

But instead of that it was a life saver with which he had come in contact, in the shape of a cumbrous but apparently watertight sea chest, which was tossing idly on the water, now rising to the crest of a billow and the next minute lost to sight in the trough of the sea. A rope was knotted about its center, which the half-drowned lad gripped with the strength of despair; and although the waves carried him up and down, down and up, as if he were so much driftwood, they did not loosen his hold.

Blinded by the spray, nearly choked by the brine, and numbed by the cold and exposure of that terrible day and night, Paul yet refused to be shaken off, and the first streak of dawn discovered him very weak and almost exhausted, but still clinging to his strange life preserver.

As soon as it was light enough to distinguish objects, he peered eagerly around for a glimpse of the Koturah. But the wreck was nowhere to be seen and even the coastline was only a thin, hazy streak in the distance. When Paul was knocked off the rigging he fell on that side of the ship facing seaward, so instead of being presently dashed on the rocks he was carried out to sea. The farther he drifted the calmer became the waves, which were now so quiet that he had no difficulty in retaining his perch on the empty chest. But his strength was almost gone, and unless help arrived very soon the plucky lad felt he could never survive the exposure of another night.

Again and again his weary eyes anxiously scanned the ocean for the welcome sight of a sail. Drifting into a comparatively smooth stretch of water, Paul cautiously stood erect on the chest and from the higher elevation renewed his eager search. Afar off on the horizon a white speck caught his eye. Kneeling on his queer craft for better security he watched the speck for fifteen minutes and saw it gradually but surely enlarge on his vision. Then he knew it was a ship, and by the progress she was making he felt certain her course lay directly toward him.

For two hours he kept his eyes fixed on that white spot, which grew larger and larger as the vessel bowled along under a favorable breeze. And yet how slowly she seemed to travel to the anxious watcher! At times he could barely restrain himself from quitting his faithful chest and plunging headlong to meet her. Supposing she should miss him after all! Oh, how his heart sunk at the thought. Then his old spirit revived. Tearing off his singlet he waved it aloft and

ADRIFT ON A QUEER RAFT.

shouted again and again until his worn-out vocal chords rebelled and utterly refused to do further duty.

But what matter! The lookout on the ship had spied him and in a delirium of joy Paul realized he was saved. With wild, staring eyes he watched the schooner set back her sails, and in a few minutes a boat was lowered manned by four stout sailors. How they pulled! The boy shrieked with delight as they flew across the water to where he knelt awaiting their approach.

Then everything became blurred. He felt a strong hand grasp him and lift him into the boat and rough but kindly voices ply him with questions. But he was past all answers. His physical powers, so long taxed beyond endurance, suddenly collapsed, and it was a dead weight which the sailors raised to the deck of the Southern Cross, a small trading schooner bound for Melbourne with a cargo of sundries.

For over a week Paul lay in the bunk where they had tenderly carried him, his brain on fire, his mind dwelling constantly on the horrors of the shipwreck. Meantime Captain Wilson, the kind-hearted skipper, gave the lad the very best attention in his power, a rude knowledge of medicine proving of no slight advantage in effecting a double rescue, for there were times when it seemed to be just a toss-up for his life. The day Port Philip Heads were sighted Paul regained consciousness and learned for the first time the name of the vessel that had picked him up and her destination. He had just strength enough to thank the captain for his kindness, and then he fell into a sound sleep, which lasted twenty-four hours. When he awoke the Southern Cross was fast to the wharf in Sandridge harbor.

All that Paul had on when he was rescued was a pair of blue serge trousers and a gray undershirt, but the thoughtful kindness of the skipper had forestalled the lad's necessities, so that, when he felt strong enough to go ashore, a neat suit of clothes brought down from Melbourne lay on a chair awaiting his occupation. Beyond telling the captain his name and that he was a survivor of the Koturah, Paul had not been very communicative, his weak condition being ample reason for withholding details. He had neither the ambition nor the heart in his enfeebled state to dilate upon the sad particulars, yet he felt it his duty to tell Captain Wilson all he knew, and this he promised to do in the presence of the company's agents at Melbourne.

Before quitting the ship, however, he outlined the story of the wreck to his new friend, dwelling particularly on Captain Barrett's message to the owners, which he was so anxious should be delivered. "Poor Barrett! Poor Barrett!" sighed the skipper when he heard of the dead man's last request. "He meant well and he stuck to his ship like a true sailor, even if he did make a big blunder. Oh, what a pity he fooled away those precious hours in trying to make the shore."

Paul was too weak to go up town that day, but on the following morning he thought he was well enough to try it. A small sum of money had been raised for him by the generous sailors and as he was anxious to make a few purchases he parted from the captain near the steamship office after promising to be back inside of an hour. There were queer pains in his head and back and as he passed slowly along Bourke street he almost wished he had asked the captain to accompany him on his shopping expedition. Whether he had overtaxed his strength or the fever, only partially checked, suddenly reappeared, Paul never knew, but presently his head grew dizzy, the buildings began to assume strange and startling shapes and he became possessed of the notion that they were just awaiting a chance to topple over and crush him.

To escape from this impending danger was his chief desire and out toward the open highway he hurried, staggering along as fast as his weak limbs would carry him. Before an iron-grated door let into a stone wall the fever-stricken lad finally dropped unconscious, and there he lay unobserved for nearly an hour, with a semi-tropical sun beating down on his head. At the end of that time a smart trap rolled up and stopped and two pleasant-featured men alighted.

"Hello, doctor?" cried the older gentleman, "what's this?"

The surgeon thus addressed stooped and attentively examined the prone figure before the gate.

"A bad case of typhoid, I should say," he presently replied in a grave voice. "Better take him inside, hadn't we?"

"My dear fellow," retorted the other, "just as you say. It isn't exactly in our line, but common humanity suggests that course, I should think."

Then they pulled the bell sharply and a servitor in livery responding he was brusquely ordered to convey Paul's limp figure into the hospital ward and have the nurses take charge of the case at once.

The doctor was quite right in his diagnosis. It was a dangerous attack of typhoid fever that had seized Paul and only by the very best of treatment was he able to pull through. But it was a long, tedious illness that he experienced and when at length he was able to crawl about in the sunny grounds few would have recognized in his pale features and emaciated figure the former sturdy sailor boy of the City of Sydney.

Six wearisome weeks had elapsed since the good doctor had found Paul unconscious at the hospital gate. At least Paul supposed it was a hospital so long as he remained in the sick ward, but when he was convalescent and able to be out doors he learned the real nature of the place in which he had found shelter. The good Samaritan who had tended him so assiduously was the house surgeon in a large private hospital for the insane, and it was to the gate of this asylum that Paul's erratic steps had carried him. The doctor explained all this to the boy the day before he gave him permission to stroll about the grounds.

"You will probably meet some queer characters out in the garden, my lad," he remarked as he stroked his long, brown beard, while a quizzical smile lit up his features, "but don't mind them; they are quite harmless. You see, this is a home for insane people, and not a mere hospital, as you supposed. Don't let that disturb you, however. In two weeks you will be well enough to leave, and then I shall lose my only sane patient."

"Yes, doctor, and he'll be sorry enough to part from one who has been so good to him," returned Paul fervently. And to think you barely know my name," he added.

"Oh, yes I do, you are number thirteen, unlucky thirteen," laughed the surgeon. "As to your real name, what matter? You say it is Paul Travers, that you are a stranger in the colonies and an American by birth. All right, when I go over to your country I'll look you up and then you can show me how ungrateful you can be, eh?"

"If you'll only give me the chance," exclaimed his patient, and as the doctor smiled good-naturedly and held out his hand Paul took the strong, white fingers in his own weak clasp. The pressure, gentle though it was, told the physician that the lad was by no means insensible of the great debt he owed to his preserver.

One week in the beautiful garden worked wonders in Paul's color and in putting flesh on his bones. It also brought him into close relations with the poor demented creatures who roamed in that earthly paradise with scarcely any appreciation of the charms of their surroundings.

Kings and princes, dukes, earls, lords, judges, generals and other titled personages innumerable met daily in the vine-covered arbors or strolled aimlessly along the graveled walks, which were bordered with richly-hued flowers and luxuriant tropical plants. All were full of absurd conceits and whimsical notions that would have been extremely ludicrous had they not been so pitiful. Paul's earliest acquaintance was a benignant, white-haired old gentleman whose peculiarity lay in fancying himself to be the Almighty. He was ever searching for his dear and only son, and his bland features were the first to greet the lad when he entered the garden. Stepping up to Paul, in a soft-spoken voice he inquired with the greatest solicitude if his dearly beloved had at last come back to his father.

"Don't enter into any argument with them," had been the doctor's final caution; "it only irritates the poor wretches. Just smile and accede to anything and everything." So Paul bowed his head in acknowledgment of the imposed honor, and was passing on when the old gentleman whispered: "So strange that you should have stayed away so long. I have needed you sorely at times, my son, but we can arrange matters for the entire universe now." Then he went over to a rustic bench and wrote industriously on a paper tablet, meantime keeping faithful watch of Paul's movements. The lad soon grew tired and made his way back to the wicket. Just as he rang the bell, the old fellow sidled up, and with an air of great mystery slipped a folded note into Paul's coat pocket, retiring quickly with his finger to his lip as an attendant appeared.

While resting on a lounge in the surgeon's office the lad brought to light the scrap of paper. On the outside was scrawled:

"God is love. Staff Sergeant William Topping, God Almighty, Melbourne." Inside was inscribed the following queer jumble:

God is love and motherless. Staff Sergeant William Topping, God Almighty. Two is company, three is none. Dear brothers and sisters, be kind, be kind to the breath of life. Bless the queen and all little children. I mend clocks and watches, hearts and souls and breathe life into the new born babe. I am God Almighty; this is my home. There is no place like home, where the birds are singing gaily and there is no place like home. Do not fear the devil, he is my worst enemy.

Paul could not help laughing over this strange hodge-podge, and yet he felt a deep sympathy for the noble-looking old man, who, the doctor said, had been at one time a well-known Melbourne merchant. Five years before his wife and only son had been wrecked almost in sight of Port Philip Heads while on a voyage back from England, and the blow had been too severe for his brain, already overburdened by business troubles. He went hopelessly crazy and had been confined in the asylum ever since.

It was a strange world in which to struggle back to life and health, and but for the cheery talks with his good friend, the house surgeon, the lad might have had a sorry time while convalescing. But his sense of humor was nicely poised and the oddity of the situation helped him through. He cheerfully lent himself to every new freak that seized his companions and then treasured his experience to recount to the doctor at their next meeting.

Paul had made such progress in the good graces of the resident surgeon that the two became quite confidential, or as much so as a lad of seventeen could expect to be with a man of forty. Up to this time the boy had avoided all mention of the wreck; but one evening, shortly before the day set for his discharge, Paul told his friend the story of the loss of the Koturah and the part he had played in that awful tragedy of the sea.

The doctor heard the lad through without comment, although an intensely interested listener. Then excusing himself for a few minutes he went up to his private room and presently returned with a bundle of newspapers. Suspecting from the doctor's manner they contained a reference to the wreck and possibly to himself, Paul eagerly took the proffered package and in a very short time had lighted upon a graphic story of "The Loss of the Koturah" as described to a representative of the Melbourne Argus by Tom Carey, who, it will be remembered, swam through the surf to shore after leaping from the boat sent out in charge of Mr. Riley, the second officer.

Carey spoke of his efforts to obtain relief on the desolate coast and his long tramp to the nearest settlement, where he succeeded in inducing half a dozen men to return with him to the beach, where they were utterly powerless to render aid. He told of their finding a half-drowned wretch who had escaped from the first officer's boat when the blind roller tossed the crew into the treacherous surf and who was the only man that managed to get ashore alive. Their long vigil on the beach while momentarily expecting the vessel to go to pieces was thrillingly portrayed; also the starting of the bonfires and of the flashlights thrown upon the survivors on the wreck.

It was almost 3 o'clock in the morning, he judged, when the Koturah made her last plunge and slipped backward from the reef under the turbulent waves, which at daylight covered every vestige of the wreck except one of the topmost spars. Although they patrolled the shore constantly, keeping a sharp lookout for possible survivors, no one managed to struggle through alive, and it was not until the day following that the bruised and swollen bodies of the victims were washed ashore.

In another column Paul read with a feeling of deep thankfulness that the second officer, with his crew, had pulled out to sea in safety, and was picked up by the vessel whose futile efforts to reach the wreck had destroyed the hopes of those left on board the Koturah. The captain's body was recovered, that of the second engineer, the old minister, Paul's little golden-haired charge and a number of others whose descriptions he recognized, including that of his poor chum, Davy. All had been removed to the settlement, twenty miles inland, and given decent burial. Out of a total of nearly two hundred passengers and crew, Carey and the survivor from the first officer's boat, together with Riley and his crew, were all that escaped—nine out of two hundred.

Paul let the papers drop to the floor and buried his face between his hands, too overcome to read further. Meantime the doctor sat stolidly puffing at his briarwood, but never taking his eyes off his young friend, whose connection with the wreck he had shrewdly suspected long before Paul gave him his confidence. Dr. Tolman had developed a great liking for the lad, whom he had snatched from the very jaws of death, and since his discovery of the shocking experience through which his protegé had passed this feeling was greatly intensified.

Waiting until Paul's fit of weeping had worn itself out, the doctor broke the rather painful silence by exclaiming: "Come, come, my boy, you must chirk up a bit or I shall have all my work to do over again. We know there was yet another saved. and now I want you to read what your friend, Captain Wilson, says, whom your absence has so greatly mystified."

CHAPTER XIV.

UNDER THE SOUTHERN CROSS.

Raising his head quickly the lad gazed with swollen eyes at the doctor, who held in his hand a folded paper which Paul had not noticed before.

"Good gracious," he exclaimed, "what a contemptible fellow he must think I am to disappear so suddenly and leave no trace when I had promised faithfully to meet him at the steamship office. And after his great kindness to me, too."

"Now, don't worry about that," interrupted the doctor. "I'll write to him in care of his agents and explain matters that will completely reinstate you in his estimation. He knew you were ill, and, like a sensible man, he probably guessed the truth, or partially so, at least. Of course, no one would think of looking for you in an insane asylum. But take this and read what he says."

The sheet was folded so that the "scare" lines heading the story caught Paul's eyes directly. The marine reporter evidently felt he had a choice morsel, and reveled in the recounting. It ran as follows:

"Captain Wilson of the Southern Cross, just in from New Zealand ports with a cargo of sundries, is responsible for a queer yarn which might be open to some doubt were it not fully corroborated by the officers and crew of his vessel. He states that a week ago last Saturday, very early in the morning, while standing direct for the Bluff, the lookout reported a man overboard on the starboard bow flying a signal of distress. A boat was lowered and the unfortunate fellow brought on board in an unconscious condition. He was a youth probably not much over seventeen, about five feet seven inches in height, well built, with dark hair and regular features. He was afloat on a seaman's chest, which, being watertight, had sustained his weight and saved his life. The lad was delirious for over a week and so exhausted when he became conscious that no one attempted to question him. During his ravings the captain gathered that the boy had been in a big wreck, from which few had escaped. When the youth was able to talk rationally he told of the loss of the Koturah and of his forced exit from the vessel just before she made her last plunge. He was reticent about giving particulars, and in fact his physical condition was such that it would have been cruel to compel him to talk. He promised, however, to go with Captain Wilson to the steamship office at Melbourne and give a detailed account of the wreck as soon as he was able.

"And now comes the queerest part of the story. Captain Wilson declares he brought the rescued lad—whose name, by the way, he gave as Paul Fraser—up from Sandridge to Melbourne. At Flinders street they separated, as Paul wished to make a few necessary purchases, but it was with the understanding that he was to meet the captain in an hour at the office of the agents of the Koturah. There Captain Wilson waited the better part of the day, but the boy failed to appear, and since then no trace of him has been discovered. As he was still very weak, it is feared that he may have had a fresh attack of fever, and in his delirious wanderings, perhaps, fell into the Yarra and was drowned."

This ended the captain's statement, but the Argus, commenting upon it, added:

"The missing lad is undoubtedly one of the crew of the ill-fated Koturah, and, what renders Captain Wilson's story doubly interesting, he is certainly the only survivor of those poor unfortunates who remained clinging to the rigging until the ship went down. It is highly important the youth should be found, not only on account of the additional facts he can give, which would be eagerly read by the relatives of the deceased passengers, as well as the general public, but also because he would prove a valuable witness before the court of inquiry now in session."

In another column of the same paper Paul found this notice:

"A reward of £20 is offered by the

proprietors of the Argus to the survivor of the Koturah who arrived at this port with Captain Wilson, on condition that he make a full and complete statement of the loss of the vessel, to be printed exclusively in this journal. He is also earnestly requested to communicate with E. O. Barrett, Ballarat, Victoria, brother of the deceased captain."

With a strange thrill at his heart Paul turned to the date line on the first page of the newspaper. It was six weeks old.

The doctor interpreted this action aright. "Yes, you are too late now, Paul," he quietly observed. "The court of inquiry has long since adjourned, and I expect Captain Wilson is cruising again in New Zealand waters by this time."

"But what were the findings of the court?" eagerly inquired the lad. "Was the captain blamed?"

"Only partially. The board, after hearing all the evidence, censured the second mate, who was in charge of the deck when the vessel struck, for neglecting to act promptly himself when the lookout reported hearing the breakers. It decided that Captain Barrett erred in trying to effect a landing on the coast instead of putting out to sea in the small boats while the opportunity existed. But, owing to his previous good record, no harsh criticism was passed on his action, and the board contented itself with simply charging him with the error of judgment. It recommended, however, that a lighthouse be built on the hidden reef, which for years has menaced the shipping, and I believe the authorities have already made the preliminary surveys for that purpose."

"And how long is it since the board adjourned?"

"A little over a month. Several detectives were sent out to seek you, but they found no clew. You see, Captain Wilson got a cargo for Hobart Town within a week, and nothing was ever said about the mistake in your name. The Argus printed it 'Fraser,' as you noticed. Perhaps Wilson forgot your right name, or maybe it was a typographical error—more likely the former, since no correction was made.

When I first read the story I suspected you right away, but a lot of good you would have done before a court of inquiry with your temperature at 104°, a pulse anywhere from 140 to 180, and a brain that was rambling of Jimmy - hit - somebody - a - whack, eye waters, dog watches, circus actors, shipwrecks, and I don't know what all besides, for two weeks at a stretch. I didn't want any court officials pottering around my patients, so I kept still and nobody is the wiser."

"It was just like you, doctor, and I'm awfully glad that I didn't have to testify. The captain's dead and gone, and the findings of the court of inquiry are pretty nearly correct anyway. But I mean to write to the owners and tell them how nobly the captain stuck to the vessel, and I'll drop a line to his brother at Ballarat. By the way, doctor, I suppose a letter to Captain Wilson in care of his agents here will reach him, won't it?"

"Oh, yes, surely, and I'll enclose one with yours, as I agreed, explaining your illness and consequent inability to keep your promise."

But the letters were not written for several days. With the pride which every Victorian takes in the magnificent capital of the colony, Dr. Tolman was eager to show Paul the beauties of Melbourne. He bore him off to the pretty suburbs of Sorrento, Brighton Beach and St. Kilda; walked him through the botanical and zoölogical gardens, showed him the handsome parliament buildings, the stately postoffice, town hall, and law courts, and then whirled him away to Williamstown to see the shipping. In short, he pointed out every feature that he thought would prove interesting to the young American, whom he treated as his honored guest.

It was at Williamstown that Dr. Tolman ran across an old friend who was the master and owner of a small schooner engaged in the island trade. Captain Viti was a half-breed Fijian, whose father, an Englishman, had in early times been attached to the British embassy at Levuka. In a joking way the skipper invited the doctor and his young friend to take a trip with him to Levuka and back.

Of course Dr. Tolman laughingly declined, but while returning to the asylum he suggested to Paul that a voyage of that nature was just the thing needed to complete a perfect cure and he urged him to accept Captain Viti's offer.

The thought of a visit to Fiji was not at all distasteful to Paul just then. Perhaps a notion of seeing the young English miss flitted across his brain, but if so he never confessed to it. The more they discussed the voyage the better he liked the idea, and next day they made a second call on the hospitable half-breed, which ended in Paul's accepting the invitation without reservation.

As the Polynesia was to sail in two days the jaunts of the doctor and his protégé were abruptly concluded, for the latter had to attend to his deferred correspondence besides laying in a supply of light clothing for the trip. These necessary articles the doctor insisted on furnishing himself. Paul still had the little purse raised by the crew of the Southern Cross, but he knew his friend would be vexed if he declined the offer, so he wisely kept still and was really grateful for the generous outfit which the doctor's kindness provided.

"Now, Paul, remember," said the good surgeon, as they stood on the deck at Williamstown just before the Polynesia cast off her mooring ropes, "if you don't get back to Melbourne write me whenever you feel like it, for I shall always be glad to hear from you. Some day, perhaps, I may get to your city of Chicago over there in America; but, pshaw! when you are editor of that big newspaper you will have forgotten all about your Australian friends."

"No, doctor, never, never," protested the lad; and then there was a last squeeze of the hand, and a last reiterated "good-bye" as the skipper called "all aboard!" and Paul had parted from another of the many good friends made on that eventful trip.

Captain Viti was an intelligent, good-natured half-breed, who proved a delightful companion on that almost idyllic voyage to Fiji. Full of interesting legends of the islands inhabited by his mother's people, he was a most entertaining talker. Hour after hour he swung idly in his hammock, adjoining Paul's, pouring tales of early missionary days into the youngster's ears that fairly made the lad's hair curl. Having lived almost entirely among the British residents at Levuka and Suva he spoke excellent English, so there were no drawbacks to the thrilling stories he recited. Under an awning stretched above their hammocks on the afterdeck the two passed most of their time, for the weather was perfect and the navigation of the schooner demanded but little attention from its captain.

A hat of native straw presented to him by Viti, a high-cut jacket of pongee silk, a pair of loose pajamas of the same material, and light yellow shoes were the chief features of Paul's airy costume at this period, a style of dress that was in perfect harmony with the tropical climate into which they were sailing. When Viti's stories flagged Paul drew on the stock of books given him by the doctor, and in his turn contributed to the entertainment by reading aloud until both fell asleep in their hammocks. It was the quintessence of laziness, this life they led, so that by the time Levuka was reached Paul's figure had regained its wonted robustness, and the lad was every whit as strong as before his illness.

There was one disappointment in store for him. Viti had explained to his guest that the English embassy was no longer quartered at Levuka, but at Suva, on a neighboring island, whither the seat of government had been transferred by Sir Arthur Gordon some time previous. The major portion of the Polynesia's cargo was intended for Levuka, where Viti owned a coffee plantation, an inheritance from his father. At this port he expected to make only a short stay, as he was anxious to get back to Sydney with a load of coffee beans which he hoped to sell at the prevailing high prices. He thought he would remain a week on shore at his plantation, and on the return trip he planned to touch at Suva, where he told Paul he might possibly have a chance to pay his respects to the little English miss.

Entering the reef-bound harbor of Levuka late in the afternoon, the schooner dropped her anchor close to shore and within a cable's length of a fringe of palms, between the openings of which Paul caught a glimpse of the brown roofs of the native huts, nestling cozily on the sides of the wooded hills which formed a bold background to the settlement. It was too late to go ashore that night, but everybody was astir early next morning, and after spending the forenoon in giving instructions to his agents regarding the disposition of his cargo, Viti was ready to start for the interior.

The road to the plantation passed through a wonderfully fertile valley in a high state of cultivation, where cocoanuts, bananas and guava fruit were as plentiful as the palm trees, which everywhere luxuriated. Birds of gayest plumage flitted overhead and eyed the travelers curiously as they jogged along on a native buckboard which Viti had borrowed from an acquaintance in the village.

Everything was deliciously novel and attractive to the young American, whose exclamations of delight were the source of much quiet amusement to his companion. During the whole of his stay on the plantation Paul was in a chronic state of mental exhilaration. Every day Viti had something new and startling to show the lad, who never tired of the long tramps and excursions planned by the energetic captain, in whose frame the spirit of his English sire largely prevailed.

But all good things have an ending, and so the order to return to the coast came one morning, as Paul knew it inevitably must. As souvenirs of his visit he carried off two big war clubs, several shell necklaces, two or three native idols and fetiches and a few other trinkets of like character, which had been pressed on him by the good-natured natives living on Viti's plantation. Loaded with his trophies, he stepped on board the trim little Polynesia with a happy heart, and after stowing away his plunder spent a pleasant evening ashore with an English missionary, who had sent a special invitation to come and drink tea at his cottage.

Next day the schooner was ready to sail away with her coffee and spices, and as the stalwart natives stood by with laughing eyes and glistening teeth to wish them a pleasant and prosperous voyage Paul could not help wondering if these jolly-looking islanders ever did have an undue fondness for white man—broiled. He preferred to think the cannibalistic stories were all myths.

At Suva, to his intense chagrin, he learned that Miss Edith and her mamma were away in the interior on a visit, which fact materially detracted from the enjoyment he had expected to derive during the few hours spent on shore. But he soon forgot his disappointment when back on the Polynesia, for the weather continued perfect, and under that blue sky it was impossible to remain long in the dumps.

The run back to Sydney was accomplished all too quickly, and when, for the second time, Paul saw on either side the stately heights of Port Jackson Heads he almost regretted that the voyage could not have been indefinitely prolonged.

By the urgent request of Captain Viti he continued to make the Polynesia his headquarters while she remained in the harbor. Resisting the importunities of the hospitable half-breed to take a run over to Hobart Town, he waited until the schooner had discharged her cargo and was ready to drop down the bay. Then taking a final farewell of her worthy owner, he stacked his belongings in a cab down on the circular quay and, with the audacity of a youngster having £5 in his pocket, ordered the driver to take him up to the Royal Hotel, on George street.

Contrary to his expectations he found no mail awaiting him this time at the postoffice. The omission caused him to remember that he had directed his people to write in care of his uncle at Adelaide, South Australia, a visit to whom Paul had planned when in New

Zealand, some time before he quitted the circus. One of his first acts after arriving in Sydney was to mail a long letter to Mr. Wilder, which he had written on board the Polynesia.

In this letter Paul described the voyage to Levuka, his experiences while on the island, and the visit to Suva, the headquarters of the British embassy. He told his story in a chatty, colloquial style, enlivening the pages with spirited sketches of native characters, and ending with a vivid description of a war dance he had witnessed on Viti's plantation, which the Fijians had given solely for his entertainment. After reading the letter over very carefully the lad was moderately certain that what he had written deserved to be designated "good stuff," in newspaper parlance, and that it would find favor in Mr. Wilder's eyes he fervently prayed.

That was not the only article he sent, either, for a week or two later he met with some rather trying personal experiences which he rightly concluded would prove excellent material for an amusing Sunday story in the Mercury. And they did, too, but it was many months before Paul was to ascertain that fact.

Living on the fat of the land at a high-priced hotel was not the wisest policy for an impecunious stranger in a foreign land to pursue. A week's diversion brought him up with a sharp turn, but before that occurred he had managed to make a number of excursions to points of interest contiguous to Sydney. A trip to the Heads in the steamer Ly-ee-Moon was among his pleasantest memories. Following that his fancy led him up the Parramatta river to Pye's Grove, along a stretch of water famous as the racing course of all the great Australian oar contests. One day his erratic steps directed him to Botany Bay, once the dumping ground for Britain's convicts, but now a popular resort for the colonials, who, on week days and Sundays, enjoy open-air concerts and light refreshments within a stone's throw of the spot where Capt. Cook landed that eventful day in April, 1770, as is faithfully recorded on a brass tablet there affixed.

In the lovely botanical gardens the lad spent many enjoyable hours. The magnificent specimens of flora and the still rarer collection of fauna indigenous to Australasia possessed powerful attractions for him, so that he never tired of the green parks, beautiful shade trees, glorious flowers, and interesting zoölogical display, which combined charms prove equally alluring to thousands of colonials who, on Sundays particularly, roam at will through the grounds.

CHAPTER XV.

RUSTLING IN THE COLONIES.

On one of these rambling days of ease, Paul paid a visit to the government dry dock at Cockatoo Island in the lower bay. Accompanied by a young middy, whose acquaintance he had formed, the lad pulled over to the island, where the vised bit of paper presented by his companion proved an open sesame to the entire place.

About the first object of interest to hold his attention was the hull of the old Alert of arctic fame, lying high and dry on the stocks, undergoing repairs, preparatory to entering the coast survey service. A queer sensation crept over the boy as he gazed on this historical craft, for it recalled an episode of his school days that he had almost forgotten.

It was the same Alert which the British government afterward tendered the United States for use in the

Greeley relief expedition under Commodore Schley, and whose stout wooden ribs had been subjected to many a nip in the icepack in the Sir George Nares arctic expedition in 1875. There was the least tinge of excitement in the lad's voice as he pointed toward her and remarked: "I was once crazy to go up in the regions that made her famous. I reckon my bones might have been picked clean by a polar bear long ago if it hadn't been for the unfortunate captain of the Jeannette."

"How was that?" demanded the middy.

"Well, it's a silly story, I suppose," laughed Paul, "but I was fairly wild to join Captain De Long's expedition to the north pole, and unknown to my people wrote several times to the commander begging him to give me a berth in the Jeannette. The first three letters I sent brought no replies, but the fourth fetched him, and also effectually dwarfed my ambition for arctic voyaging. Of course there was no good reason why I should encumber the expedition, and that is the way Captain De Long viewed the matter. I remember very distinctly every word in that short, terse letter he sent me. It was dated New York, April 1, 1879, and his address, I recollect, was 150 West 11th street. Here is what it said:

PAUL TRAVERS, ESQ.—*Sir:* Your various letters have been received. In reply I would state that I have room in the Jeannette for nobody but her officers and crew. These must be seamen or people with some claim to scientific usefulness and unless you can be classed with either party I cannot possibly take you.

"Was that all?"

"No, it was signed, 'Very respectfully, George W. De Long, lieutenant, commanding arctic steamer Jeannette.'"

Paul's friend whistled reflectively. "Pretty chilly note, that," he said. "Colder than Siberia itself, I should say. I suppose you have never bragged much of your correspondence, have you?"

"No-o, not for a good while," admitted the lad, ruefully. "But I kept the letter, though, and when news came to America of the awful disaster that overtook the Jeannette and her brave commander I hunted it up, and without saying a word gave it to my father to read. Of course the whole story had to be told them, and there was great rejoicing among the women folks over what they called my fortunate escape."

"Never thought much of those north pole fanatics," exclaimed the ingenuous young sailor. "My dad's a second cousin or something of Sir John Franklin, and he's always praising the old chap up to the skies, but between you and me I think Sir John was a chump. It's only another form of lunacy, this north pole pioneering. What's to be gained if a fellow does discover an open polar sea? 'Twon't do commerce any good, will it? Or open up any new summer resorts and things like that? Bah! I've no use for your would-be arctic explorers, who are always fitting out expeditions and then hanging on by their eyebrows up yonder in the frozen regions waiting for a rescuing party to come along and carry home their remains." After which forcible but frank expression of opinion the energetic middy let his hand fall with a resounding thwack on Paul's back, which brought that idle dreamer up "all standing."

Two days after this experience the landlord of the Royal Hotel sent Paul a polite but peremptory note and a bill, the size of which staggered the young American. To pay it would take nearly every penny he had, but, as the demand was imperative, to settle it and get away was the only honorable course.

That night he rented a cot bed at a cheap hotel in a most unfashionable quarter of the town, and next morning started out in earnest to "rustle for a grub stake," as he eloquently expressed it. True to his philosophy, he had played the elegant gentleman to a finish as long as his money lasted, and was now ready to try the other tack for a while.

It wasn't pleasant, though, to find himself with empty pockets again, and the first day Paul almost repented the prodigality of the preceding fortnight. But the sale of a pair of cuff buttons and several other trinkets furnished him enough funds to keep the wolf off for two or three days, during which time he assiduously canvassed the town for work. Rebuffed everywhere, he was on his way down Pitt street the third morning when the sight of the Sydney Herald building suggested that he apply inside for a position.

Inquiring for the managing director, Paul expressed his desire for employment on the paper. For a few moments the lad feared the great newspaper man would have an apoplectic fit when he finally grasped the sense of this modest request. But the magnate rallied and in a pompous tone informed the presumptuous youth that the management of the Herald usually selected its staff when it needed reenforcement and that it never opened its doors to impecunious strangers. He looked so shocked when he made this announcement that Paul was sure he had grieved the editor, and he humbly apologized for the intrusion. As he backed out he politely asked if he might see the advertisements in the morning paper. The great man shot a withering glance over his glasses and curtly observed that the advertisements could be found posted on the bulletin board down stairs.

Paul crawled out feeling very cheap and insignificant and approached the blackboard, before which stood a number of fellows, who, like himself, were trying to get track of work. He edged in and scanned the list of "wants" carefully, but it didn't seem to be a good morning for likely situations. There were several appeals for market gardeners, a healthy demand for experienced coachmen, one or two requests for London-bred footmen of fine appearance, and a solitary invitation for a "pious young Protestant to make himself useful in a Christian family" where two other servants were kept. But none of these seemed to be full of promise. The only one that offered any encouraging prospect read as follows:

> WANTED—A YOUNG MAN OF PLEASING address and some business tact to solicit orders for a new ink. Call at 97 Lower George street, before 11 o'clock.

"Pleasing address," reflected Paul.

"Well, I have no business to hail from Chicago if I can't count that as one of my accomplishments. Don't know about the business tact; guess I'll have to risk that."

It lacked a few minutes of 11, but Lower George street was not far away, so Paul quickly repaired to the given number. He found the ink manufacturer at work in a dirty back room, whence issued a most villainous smell. As the lad entered the man wiped his deeply stained fingers on a streaked apron and with a pronounced cockney accent asked what was wanted.

"I have called in answer to your advertisement in the Herald for a young man to solicit orders for ink."

"Ow! I si; you never sowld hink before, naow, 'ave you?"

"No, sir; but I've used lots of it, and can tell a good brand when I see it."

"Think of that, naow! Well, 'ow d'ye laike this?" And he shoved a big can of vile-smelling liquid under the nose of his visitor.

With rare presence of mind Paul forced a smile and assured the proprietor it seemed to be the right stuff, and hoped it was the ink he wanted sold. This subtle flattery had its effect and after some further parley Paul was taken on trial, a liberal commission being promised on all sales he should make. His pockets were then filled with tiny sample bottles of the "Cologne Kaiser-Tinte Fluid," in addition to which homeopathic doses he was given a bundle of printed circulars exploiting the commercial value of the famous Kaiser-Tinte. The Englishman next directed his new solicitor to first visit all the colleges and private schools in the city, where sample bottles and circulars were to be left and orders taken whenever possible.

Just before receiving his final instructions Paul suggested that an advance of two shillings on his possible commissions would be very acceptable, owing to the state of his finances. The cockney demurred and at first refused point blank, but on Paul's assurance that he would put in a hard day's work the grimy manufacturer relented and compromised on a shilling. He then followed the lad to the door and urged him to devote all his energy to pushing the Kaiser-Tinte.

Paul wore the light suit of clothes which Captain Wilson had bought for him in Melbourne. He felt a little nervous, as he walked gingerly along George street, for fear of breaking the sample bottles, which bulged out of his pockets and flapped against his hips with each step he took. The day was warm and the exercise unusual, so that by the time he had called at a dozen schools and colleges without obtaining an order his temper was the least bit ruffled. The colonial Australian is very like his English first-cousin—not particularly affable toward strangers and inclined to haughtiness and arrogance in the treatment of his social inferiors.

Paul's feelings were severely lacerated on more than one occasion that day, and it was really quite pathetic to see him meekly retire when a supercilious preceptor sharply requested him to "go away with the nawsty stuff and don't bother."

But the young solicitor followed the instructions of his principal faithfully, and, although unsuccessful, he called on all the saints in Sydney in regular rotation. St. Andrew's, St. James', St. Leonard's, St. Luke's, St. Mark's, St. Michael's and St. Phillip's—all flouted him and would have none of his wares. Paul was in despair; he concluded that he lacked the requisite "business tact" announced in the advertisement, for not a single order could he secure. Totally discouraged, he finally introduced himself to the "head master" of a college on Castlereagh street and, placing two or three sample bottles on his desk, politely handed him a circular.

The pedagogue eyed Paul suspiciously, and picking up a ruler made a lunge at the lad's knuckles, fortunately missing his mark.

"I pelief you vas a sneak tief!" he exclaimed. "I vos pin loogin' for you! Uf you dond ged righd oud I gif yu in sharge uf der boliss. Here, Zollomon, pud dis fellow oud!"

Solomon approached. He was evidently the servitor of the institution; a dull, heavy-eyed man, with big hands and large, clumsy feet. He dropped an immense paw on Paul's shoulder, gave him a rough push, which was feebly resented, and trotted his prisoner across the graveled campus toward the outer gates. The lad was so angry he could have killed his captor with exquisite satisfaction to himself, but he was as helpless as a child in the grasp of such a Cerberus. As they neared the gate a scheme for revenge darted through Paul's brain, which he put into execution the minute he was released. Just as Solomon gave him a final farewell push the lad drew the cork from one of his sample bottles, and let his tormentor have a dose of "Kaiser-Tinte" full in the face. Then he sprinted up Castlereagh street as hard as he could run, with the big servitor behind shouting "Stop tief" at the top of his lungs.

But Solomon was not built for rapid transit and he was soon distanced. Slackening his speed now that he was safe from pursuit, Paul was about to turn off on Pitt street when his foot tripped on the uneven curbing and he fell heavily on the stone pavement.

PEDDLING "KAISER TINTE" IN SYDNEY.

Luckily, no bones were broken, but, alas! about all of his sample bottles were, and as the dispirited ink solicitor picked himself up he felt several independent streams chasing down the inside of his trousers, while numerous dark stains on the outside told the harrowing truth.

His light suit of clothes was streaked with dark-blue stripes, his body was badly bruised, and his spirits were so depressed that for a few seconds after he pulled himself together it was a toss-up whether he wouldn't boo-hoo right out in the public street. But by swallowing hard he kept the tears back, and, looking like an animated war map, sought the ink manufacturer and resigned his commission. Then came the crowning injury. The man not only demanded a return of the shilling he had advanced, but had the temerity to want pay for the broken sample bottles, and threatened to hand the lad over to the police if he didn't produce the money instantly.

As Paul had spent the shilling for dinner this was an impossibility. "I haven't a cent to my name," he exclaimed with some heat, "and if I had you'd have to take it out of my hide before I'd pay a nickel. The bottles were broken accidentally and the shilling I have earned ten times over."

"Don't give me h'any of your sauce, boy," retorted the cockney. "You're a sharper like h'all h'other h'Americans. Get h'out of 'ere!" And seizing the lad by the shoulders he roughly pushed him through the doorway into the corridor, whence Paul found the street.

A bath in the Parramatta river removed most of the ink stains, but no amount of soaking would take the streaks out of his clothes. He was a marked youth.

Hungry and disheartened, Paul returned to his lodgings, only to find that one of the occupants of the common room had walked off with his valise. This was the climax. He hadn't a penny to pay for the cot privilege over night, nor any courage left to ask for credit. As he hurried out in the gathering gloom of the streets, after a long but vain search for the lost satchel, a few salty tears welled up, and, though he brushed them hastily off, a fresh supply insistently appeared. Dark days had fallen on the young traveler.

His bunk that night was on the soft side of a bench in Cook park, on his favorite seat under the statue of the great circumnavigator. At 4 o'clock the next morning he was astir to avoid the appearance of the park police, who had an unpleasant habit of running in all vagrants caught napping at that hour. Rinsing his face and hands in the artificial lake, Paul utilized his one lone handkerchief as a towel and then strolled back to his seat to wait for sunrise. While disconsolately kicking the gravel and wondering by what possible means he could obtain breakfast a young fellow with a week's old beard, who lounged on an adjoining bench, accosted him.

"Hello, son; you don't look happy this morning!"

"Not very," returned Paul, who recognized one of his own countrymen by the speaker's accent. "I'm broke."

"Is that all?" was the half scornful rejoinder. "Why, I've been broke many a time; that's what proves a man. It's no trick to get along when you have money in your pockets; any fool can spend money."

"Yes; I've discovered that. But it isn't a bad thing to have when a fellow's hungry. Where are you from?"

"'Frisco, last. Folks live up in Michigan—place called Grand Rapids; mebbe you've heard of it."

"Oh, yes; that's where they make furniture, isn't it?"

"You bet! Any amount of it. Used to work in a chair factory myself, but I hated the steady grind and took to the road; been driftin' around for three years, and am mighty tired of it, too."

"Then why not go back?"

"I mean to, soon 's I make a stake; hate to go there without a sou after knockin' about for three years. Where do you call home?"

"Chicago!"

"Windy City, eh? That's a burg I'm stuck on. If I ever get back to the states, you'll see me headed for that town, sure. It's a Jim Dandy place for a young fellow, 'cordin' to my notion. But say, let's mosey along and get some breakfast. I've got just a shillin' left and we'll blow it in for two square meals. Come on, Chicago."

Paul's new companion answered to the name of Jim. He was a cheery sort of a fatalist, with a droll manner of speech that was not without its charms. Among other of his many accomplishments he could imitate bird calls very cleverly by means of a little tin contrivance dubbed a bird whistle, which is placed on the tip of the tongue when in action.

Jim had a notion he could manufacture these whistles in quantities so they could be sold to the colonials in the Saturday night market place. The project did not appear at all feasible to Paul when it was first broached, for, as he observed, "how could they get the necessary materials when neither had a cent of capital?"

But Jim was a young man of wonderful resources. After he had decided the scheme was worth trying, he instructed his companion to visit the various shoemakers and harness shops in town and beg scraps of leather while he made a tour of the alleys collecting discarded tin cans. Both were fairly successful and loaded with their spoils the two adventurers met at noon at the rendezvous by Capt. Cook's statue, where Jim at once began operations.

He was a genius. With the aid of a jack-knife and the slight assistance Paul could render, thirty "illigant bird whistles," as Jim termed them, were ready for possible customers when the chimes sounded 6 o'clock. The artisans were by this time both tired and hungry, but their Saturday night supper as well as their Sunday dinner depended on their success at the market. With such an incentive the embryo merchants were not long in reaching the inclosure where Cheap Johns of every description reveled.

CHAPTER XVI.

EXPERIENCES IN THE ANTIPODES.

The Saturday night market is one of the institutions of Sydney. It is held in an inclosed square at the lower end of Pitt street, and by paying a small entrance fee the petty merchant is entitled to exhibit and sell his wares. It is the poor man's paradise, where anything in the household line may be purchased, and where the good wife may do her week's marketing at a minimum cost. It is also a popular resort for the colonial 'Arry and his best girl, who flock there in great numbers to patronize the side-shows, round-abouts, Aunt Sallys, quack doctors, lemonade peddlers, oyster stands, and electric-try-your-nerve-machines. This kaleidoscopic scene is thrown into high relief by means of numerous oil lamps, whose odor is not of the pleasantest, but which, to the habitual patron, is one of the charms of the market.

Arrived at the gate, the entrance fee of "thruppence," or six cents, was obtained by a quick sale outside to a willing victim, who was easily captured by Jim's artistic exhibition of the possibilities of a bird whistle. An empty box had been picked up on the way, and once inside the grounds a good site was soon selected in the vicinity of a popular quack doctor. Here Jim mounted the box and by his beautiful delineations quickly attracted a crowd. While he warbled Paul extolled the whistles and explained what a delightful accomplishment was within the reach of anybody who had a spare "thruppenny-bit" to invest. Each did his part so well that in an hour the stock was exhausted, and after dividing the receipts the partners found they could indulge in two meals a day, at least, for the ensuing week.

It seemed good to crawl into a sure-enough bed once more, and it was not until the bells were chiming for church next morning that Paul awoke. A day of complete rest without the disturbing problem of meals to worry him prepared the lad for a week of steady work, every day of which was devoted to the new industry of manufacturing bird whistles. It is hardly necessary to say that the skilled labor was furnished by Jim, while Paul rustled for material, in which line he was highly successful.

By the Saturday following the partners had finished nearly a gross of whistles which they planned to unload on the colonials. An ingenious circular written by Paul and printed on sixteenth - sheets purported to explain succinctly how to imitate the various bird-calls, and one of these was wrapped around every whistle. With the opening of the gates the expectant pair marched in and quickly drew a gaping crowd. Paul had rehearsed a very effective lecture explanatory of the various calls imitated, the pauses being filled by Jim, who demonstrated the correctness of his partner's statements, in an entirely satisfactory manner. It was during these rests, so to speak, that Paul drove a brisk trade, the lecture and trilling being repeated as often as the crowd changed or business waned.

By closing time every whistle was sold. Intoxicated with their success, and loaded with small silver, the young merchants repaired to their lodgings, where the receipts of the evening were promptly counted and divided. It was a hard grind to work the second week at whistle-making. Each had too much money in his possession to be very industrious, so that by the next market night the stock on hand was rather limited. To this day Paul is not certain whether by the most assiduous practice anyone could learn to blow the whistles they made. True, Jim was an expert, which was an argument in their favor, but then Jim did many things which no one else could successfully imitate.

It would seem that the colonials who were patronizing the young Americans had reached the conclusion that the bird-calls were rank frauds and that they had been basely imposed upon. At least this is what the partners supposed when they stopped running and could safely sum up the situation.

They had been ignominiously driven out of Eden. Paul had scarcely started his fascinating lecture when a dozen sturdy youths rushed for their stand, knocking it over and pummeling the unlucky venders in a shameful manner. It was no time to show fight; the odds were too great, and, quickly realizing that discretion was better than valor, both lads made a bee line for the nearest fence, with the howling colonials in hot pursuit. It was a pretty piece of sprinting, but the pursued reached the boards first and over the top each vaulted in beautiful style, while a cry of rage issued from the throats of the disappointed Britishers, who loudly demanded their "thruppences" back because the "beastly things wouldn't blow, ye know!"

"Blow!" remarked Jim, later on, when they discussed this extraordinary procedure, "of course they wouldn't. It's a trick of the tongue, just as you explained to 'em. But that's the ingratitude of the world. Try to teach 'em something new, and the people turn and snarl at a fellow. Ah, well, this snap couldn't last forever, I suppose," and with a philosophical shrug Jim puffed out the light of the tallow dip and plunged into bed.

Three days after this experience the reports of new gold diggings "up country" inoculated the pair with the mining fever, and in half an hour the two had decided to pool their capital, buy an outfit, and set out at once for the gold fields of which all Sydney was talking.

Their "prospector's kit" was not very elaborate, for provisions had to be included, and Jim insisted on reserving a small fund of ready cash for possible emergencies. A journey by stage coach was not to be considered on account of the extortionate fare demanded, so they determined to follow the trail afoot. As both lads were in prime condition, physically, this was not a very arduous undertaking, and until they reached the glaring, sandy stretches of country 100 miles north of Sydney each thoroughly enjoyed the novel experience of traveling through the bush. With one-third the distance covered in less than a week they felicitated themselves on their progress, when an unforeseen disaster occurred which upset all their plans.

Jim was stricken with the sand blight.

For two days following their advent into the sandy desert the older lad had complained of a pain in his eyes, succeeded by a puffing up of the inflamed cuticle, which gradually increased until two small slits were all that remained to mark the location of his eyes. The itching was intolerable, and with a scant water supply the poor fellow endured great torture. By the third day Jim's sufferings were so severe that Paul became seriously alarmed. With his comrade totally blind and little hope of immediate recovery, it was useless to think of continuing the journey; to get back to Sydney and put Jim in the hospital for treatment was clearly the only wise course, and this Paul determined to pursue.

He was lucky enough to sell their kit, at a great sacrifice, to an outgoing party that camped near by, and the sum thus obtained, added to their own reserve fund, procured two seats in the stage coach to Sydney, the return fare being much more reasonable. Poor Jim suffered agonies during the two days and a half consumed in making the trip. All that Paul could do to alleviate the pain in any degree was to apply cold cloths, but the water he carried in a bottle soon became tepid, which destroyed the efficacy of the bandages, so despite constant applications Jim experienced little relief.

But he endured the torture like a stoic, and even found courage to rally Paul on his depression, telling him that a true philosopher was the fellow who could apply his pet theories to his own misfortunes and then extract consolation. "Anybody can be a philosopher," he observed, "when the world treats him well, when his pockets are lined with cash, his health is good and three meals are coming regularly. It's when a chap's down on his luck, friends have deserted him, and the prospects for improving his condition are awfully slim that he has a good

IN THE AUSTRALIAN
GOLD FIELDS.

chance to show his nerve, or, if you like that better, his philosophy."

"Did you ever read 'Martin Chuzzlewit,' Jim?" inquired Paul, after one of these talks.

"No; Dickens wrote it, didn't he? Never read much of Dickens 'cept 'Pickwick.' I rather cottoned to Sam Weller; bright duck he was. Why?"

"Oh, nothing; you reminded me of a character in the story; that's all; fellow named Mark Tapley."

"What about him?"

"Well, he was a philosopher in his way, too. A cheerful sort of philosophy his was. Whenever things looked darkest and the prospect was particularly gloomy, Mark grew correspondingly jolly. The blacker the cloud, the more cheerful he became; nice sort of a fellow to travel with, he must have been."

"And I remind you of him, do I?" mused Jim, as a sharp twinge caused his features to suddenly contract. "Well, I reckon it's a heap sight healthier to grin than to groan, and I'll keep on grinning just as long as I can stand the racket."

The opportunity of studying a first-class case of sand blight, as the doctors called Jim's attack, was too good to miss, and the sufferer was promptly admitted when Paul took him to the hospital for examination immediately on their arrival in Sydney. As it would be many weeks, they said, before he could be cured, Paul was obliged to part company with his friend. For the first time since his illness Jim displayed signs of weakness when the lad came to the edge of the cot to say good-bye.

"I'd made up my mind to see you safe home to Chicago, young fellow," groaned the invalid, "and now the doctor says I'll be lucky if I get away from here in three months. Hopeful outlook, isn't it?" Then with a return of his old spirit he added: "Never mind, son; I'll be back there almost as soon as you are; see if I'm not. I'm not at all sure but I'll be at the head of the brass band to welcome you into town, so get a move on yourself, boy."

The cheap hotel where Paul engaged a bed was patronized pretty freely by the humbler followers of the Australian Jockey Club, the majority of whom were touters, riders and bookmakers' clerks. With one of the latter—a decent enough young fellow—Paul became acquainted, and through him was introduced to a bookmaker, who hired the lad to keep his accounts. The work was fairly easy and the pay good, but in the thirty days he remained out at the course the youngster saw just enough of the inside workings of a racing association to arouse anything but a high opinion of the turf. With the close of the season at Randwick he respectfully declined a proposition from his employer to make the circuit with him, and, drawing his wages, which were materially increased by a handsome present from the successful bookmaker, Paul abruptly ended this phase of his career.

A short time previous he had found a hotel on Castlereagh street, kept by an American, where he rented a modest room. The house was quite popular with theatrical people, and among others with whom Paul came in contact was a dapper little Frenchman named Henri L'Estrange, an aeronaut of some skill and undoubted courage. L'Estrange was under contract to make a balloon ascension from the public domain on the queen's birthday, which is always a popular holiday with the loyal colonials. His acquaintance with the professor opened up a new field of adventure for Paul. In Colorado he had been many hundred feet underground, on shipboard he had climbed as high as the topmast crosstrees permitted, but a sail in the air was an altogether novel experience which he eagerly craved.

Assiduous cultivation of the little Frenchman soon won from the aeronaut a promise to take Paul along as his assistant on the day of the fête, and until that time arrived the two were inseparable. Behind canvas walls, on the common contiguous to the botanical gardens, the "Empress of Night" was moored. For several days prior to the ascension L'Estrange and his new assistant spent many hours splicing ropes, tightening valves, sewing sand bags, painting the car, and otherwise preparing the balloon for its aerial voyage. Arrangements were made to inflate the bag from the nearest gas main, and on the morning of May 24 all was in readiness to make the attachment. The balloon was advertised to ascend at 3 p.m., and fully an hour before that time the public domain and streets adjacent were black with a holiday-making crowd.

But the Frenchman was not happy; the gas was bad, and the balloon showed no disposition to soar. "Ah, ciel!" exclaimed the little man in despair. "Zees gaas ees vair poor. Eet ees not suffissien buoy-ant; ze qualite ees execrable!"

For several hours the professor and his assistant had attempted to inflate the balloon to a satisfactory pitch. At 3 o'clock the big bag swayed in the air like a drunken man, its dropsical folds, which refused to fill out, reminding Paul of a huge pair of misfit Turkish trousers. Driven almost crazy by the demands of the mob, which, unlike an American crowd, was disposed to wax wrathy at the delay, the Frenchman jumped on a box, and, in his broken English, explained that he was quite ready and willing to fill his part of the contract, but was unexpectedly confronted with so inferior a quality of gas that it threatened to defeat the exhibition entirely.

An hour later the incessant chaffing of the spectators so worried the aeronaut that, against his better judgment, he determined to cut loose and make the ascension. Motioning Paul into the car, he sprung lightly over the side and instructed the park attendants to slip the main cable.

The Empress of Night rose slowly to the height of about fifty feet, and then, deliberately sulking in the air, refused to soar an inch more. "Ah! tees as I expected," murmured the professor, and, pulling the escape valve, the balloon descended amid the jeers of the colonials, whose quips at his expense nearly drove the Frenchman frantic. Excited and angry, he ordered Paul to jump out and in a few moments had detached the car from the rope network above. Then, with a graceful bow to the impatient spectators, the daring aeronaut jumped into the netting of the balloon, motioned the men to let go and in a minute had shot high above the heads of the now breathless colonials.

Another minute the crowd remained silent, then arose a burst of cheering which was as spontaneous as it was heartfelt, for everyone recognized the intrepidity of the act. In response to this recognition, from his perilous perch above, L'Estrange was seen to wave his cap three times before he passed beyond the direct vision of the excited watchers, who speculated freely on his chances for descending in safety.

Drifting south, the balloon lost its buoyancy and fell rapidly. Over Pitt street the bag swayed unpleasantly close to a stack of chimneys, rose and dropped again in erratic plunges, then took a sudden dash over George street, bumping viciously against a hotel building, where, ·by chance, a woman stood at an open window holding a lighted candle. In a second the escaping gas had ignited, an explosion followed, and poor L'Estrange was thrown on the glass roof of the court below, where he was picked up a few minutes later with a broken leg and arm, several fractured ribs and some severe burns as a memento of his brave but foolhardy experiment. As for Paul, this brief experience was quite enough to dampen his ardor for aeronautics, but the little Frenchman only shrugged his shoulders, when someone asked him if he would ever make another ascension, as he answered: "To-morrow, to-day, eef I vas able to pull ze r-rope!"

A few days later Paul was pleased to receive a letter bearing the Adelaide postmark, which proved to be from his mother's brother, who for thirty years had been a resident of South Australia. In it the merchant cordially invited the nephew he had never seen to visit his Australian relatives, and ended by delicately hinting that if Paul was short of funds he might draw on him for needful supplies.

Fortunately, the lad was not obliged to act on his uncle's suggestion. He still had a fair sum left from his earnings, and this he intended should cover all the expenses of his visit.

Thanking his uncle for the kind invitation, he wrote that he would follow the letter in a day or two at the farthest. As soon as L'Estrange was pronounced out of danger Paul secured a berth on the steamer Ly-ee-Moon for Melbourne, which port he reached just in time to transfer his baggage to the little Aldinga, bound for Adelaide. Disappointed of a call on Dr. Tolman, he consoled himself with the thought of a visit on his return, and, pleasantly musing over the probable appearance of his new cousins, fell asleep in his narrow berth.

A bluff, jolly looking man of fifty, with a heavy beard and kindly eyes, and a mild, sweet little woman, with a pale, intellectual face, were the two hasty silhouettes Paul caught of his uncle and aunt at dusk, as they welcomed him to their hearts and home. Two boys, about his own age, and five pretty girls, ranging from fourteen to twenty-four, comprised the junior portion of the family, with whom Paul was soon on the best of terms.

Five charming girls! All so sweet-tempered and affectionate, and quite ready to do anything to please their American cousin! What a delightful prospect for the lad who for so long had encountered chill looks and brusque words. Cricket with the boys, croquet and lawn tennis with the girls, varied with parties, picnics and excursions galore. A week at Glenelg, the Newport of South Australia, proved an idyllic experience, of which bathing, fishing and boating formed the principal features. Yachting parties were extemporized in the lad's honor, in which his fair cousins and their friends vied with one another to make each occasion more enjoyable than the preceding.

It must be confessed that among so many nice people Paul discreetly kept his rougher experiences in the background, yet he did not attempt to deny that he was traveling around the world on a very slim purse. What money he had he spent freely, although there was little that he could pay for in that generous crowd. Six weeks of this existence almost spoiled the young man for further campaigning, and it was only when his rapidly diminishing stock of cash warned him that he had barely enough to carry him back to Sydney that he resolutely broke away from his pleasant surroundings.

All seemed loath to have him go, for blood ties are strong the world over, and Paul was the only relative that had ever visited them. There were many tears shed by his fair cousins, a warm grasp from his uncle and the boys and a fervent good-bye kiss from his aunt when Paul stepped aboard the steamer City of Adelaide at the port. Through moist eyes he watched for the last flutter of handkerchiefs and for the final handwave from the warm-hearted Australians who had done so much to make his visit among them supremely happy and enjoyable. Then, with a big lump in his throat, he went below. It was time to drop the role of gentleman and resume that of a tramp again.

CHAPTER XVII.

FAREWELL TO AUSTRALIA.

Dr. Tolman greeted the young American very cordially when, unannounced, Paul walked into the physician's private office at the hospital.

"Why, my dear boy," he exclaimed, "I had about given up all hope of seeing you again. I have had just one letter since you went away. Ah, you youngsters are so fickle; the friend of a week ago is forgotten in the friend of to-day. But I'm glad to see you looking so well; sit down and give an account of yourself since we parted."

For an hour Paul entertained the doctor with the story of his trip to Fiji; his days of ease and his days of hardship at Sydney; the ink-peddling incident, bird-whistle transactions, gold-mining episode, jockey-club experience, his attempt at balloon voyaging, and last, but not least, his delightful visit among the charming South Australian cousins.

The doctor was highly amused at the graphic description Paul gave of his efforts to introduce "Kaiser-Tinte" in the collegiate circles of Sydney, and he fairly roared over the manner in which the lad avenged his insults on Solomon the servitor. Referring to the bird-whistle episode, he laughingly declared the partners deserved the drubbing administered by the young colonials, whereat Paul waxed indignant and protested it was an honest transaction, in which the Sydneyites were worsted only because they did not prove apt pupils.

"Oh, that was it," observed the doctor, dryly; "well, of course, you couldn't expect them to be as smart as two Yankees."

The succeeding week, which Paul passed with his friend, was devoted to rambles through the botanical gardens and in delightful excursions to the many charming suburbs for which Melbourne is noted. One day, toward the close of his visit, as the two sat on the bench at St. Kilda idly watching the bathers, the doctor suddenly asked Paul if he had any definite plans for getting back home.

"Yes and no," answered the lad. "I have a hope of getting a berth on one of the Orient steamers at Sydney which will carry me through to London, but whether I succeed is doubtful. Judging from past experiences, it isn't an easy matter, but having come so far 'right side up,' I'm not going to borrow trouble at this late day. After I reach London, I'll trust to luck to get to New York; that looks simple enough compared with the problem that confronts me just now."

The doctor chuckled softly. "You're a queer boy, Paul. Here you are, twelve thousand miles from home, with barely enough money to pay your fare to Sydney, and yet you are as free from care as my dog. I confess I am envious of so tranquil a disposition."

"Well, what's the good of fretting?" returned the lad. "I entered into this state deliberately and of my own free will and accord, as the lawyers say; I should be an idiot to whine over hardships and trials for which I alone am responsible. No, sir; when I get to my troubled bridges I'll cross them, but no worrying in advance if I can help it."

"Right you are, Paul; that's good, sound philosophy, and I hope you will live up to it. After all, the more experiences you get the better qualified you will be for the profession you are ambitious to enter. Let me see, how long is it since you left home?"

"Ten months—ten years, I had almost said. So much has happened in that time I can scarcely realize a year has not yet passed. I went away from Chicago a boy—perhaps more matured than the average lad of seventeen, for I had been an omnivorous reader, but the one that goes back to the bustling city on the shores of Lake Michigan will be immeasurably older. It isn't the number of years one lives," he added pensively, "but the manner in which one lives them that makes the man. I hope I shall have nothing to regret in the future when I look back on this eventful tramp."

"You won't, my lad; you won't, if

you keep yourself pure, mentally and morally," was the doctor's earnest rejoinder, "and I believe you have too much good sense to stray far off the right track."

The older man parted from Paul with genuine regret. He had taken a great fancy to the sturdy American lad whose acquaintance he had so strangely formed. As he said his last good-bye down at the dock, just as the bell warned all visitors ashore, there was a tremor in his voice which indicated the depth of his feelings. "Some day we shall meet again, my boy, so I won't say 'farewell,' but 'auf weidersehen,' as the Germans so beautifully express it." Then he slipped a sealed note into Paul's hand, and, hastily crossing the gangway, disappeared in the crowd.

In his cabin, after tea, Paul opened the letter which Dr. Tolman had so hurriedly given him at parting. It contained a brief message and a banknote to the value of £5. The lines read:

DEAR PAUL—Don't refuse the little gift I enclose, as it is merely a token of my regard for a brave young traveler who has fully demonstrated his ability to get along without money. But it will make me feel easier to know you are not penniless when you get to Sydney, so I entreat you to keep it. With deepest affection and wishing you a safe return to Chicago, I am, sincerely your friend,

HENRY BERTRAM TOLMAN.

One of the uses to which Paul put the money on his arrival at Sydney was to buy a watch charm of the famous New Zealand greenstone, on the gold mounting of which he had engraved "Paul to H. B. T. Fideliter." This he sent, with his best love, to his good friend, together with a long letter, expressing his deep appreciation of the many kindnesses he had received and which he assured the doctor he could never forget.

As he had divined, getting a berth on a London-bound steamer was by no means an easy job. For several weeks Paul haunted the circular quay, alongside which the colossal ocean steamers unload their cargoes, but, although he boarded many and assiduously cultivated the acquaintance of the understewards, he could find no opening. One after another he saw the big liners discharge their passengers and freight, fill up again and slowly steam out into the bay, bound for the port he so earnestly desired to reach.

By carefully hoarding the money which the doctor had so generously given him, he was able to live in a fairly comfortable way during this disheartening period, but as the weeks slipped by his funds grew lamentably smaller. It was his custom every morning to scan the bulletin board in front of the Herald building, in the hope of finding a situation which might tide him over until his prospects brightened. Running his eyes down the "lost and found" column one day, when he had been nearly a month in Sydney, he saw an advertisement for a lost key of peculiar shape, which the finder was requested to bring to the manager of the Queensland Bank and receive a reward.

It suddenly occurred to Paul that he had that same key in his vest pocket. The night before, while standing in front of the Royal Theater, he had seen it glistening on the pavement, and, picking it up, had stowed it away in his clothes after a cursory glance at its curious shape.

He now took it out and compared it with the description. Yes, there were the numbers, 121307, stamped in the steel, corresponding exactly with those advertised. Clearly the key belonged to the manager of the Queensland Bank, and in search of that official Paul at once bent his steps.

"You can't see the manager; he's engaged," was the somewhat curt answer which a tall young man, wearing a huge choker collar, made to Paul's polite request.

"Then I'll wait till he's disengaged," was the lad's cheerful response, plumping down into a bench placed for the convenience of bank patrons.

The owner of the collar made a sneering remark, the purport of which Paul did not catch, and resumed his work of adding a column of figures, the interruption of which had ruffled his temper.

Half an hour elapsed without the sign of a caller emerging from the manager's room. Paul began to suspect the surly clerk of tampering with the truth. "Are you sure the manager's engaged?" he suddenly ventured.

"That's what I said," was the snappish reply, "and you'll have to wait."

A few minutes later one of the employes went in to see the manager, leaving the door at such an angle that Paul's eyes could rove over the entire room. The manager was alone, save for the presence of the clerk.

The lad's ire was aroused. He was justly incensed at the uncivil treatment accorded him by the ill-bred clerk, and he fairly ached to punch the fellow's head.

Raising his voice a trifle and addressing the unmannerly youth, he exclaimed, "Excuse me, sir, but will you ask the manager to give me five minutes of his time? I want to see him on a matter of business."

Paul noticed the gray head perk up a bit in the inside room as the sound seeped through, and presently a brusque "Mr. Peters!" floated outward.

The proprietor of the tall collar unwound his long legs from the stool and, with a black look at Paul, disappeared in the private room.

In a few minutes he emerged, still wearing a scowl, and, walking over to Paul, jerked out, "he'll see you now."

"Oh, thank you," returned the lad with one of his blandest looks; "sorry to have put you to so much trouble."

He wasted no time in stating his business when he stood before the manager. "I saw your advertisement about a lost key," he began. "I found it last night in front of the Royal Theater. This is the article, I believe," and he placed the key on the banker's desk.

The manager picked it up, saw the number was correct, and said: "This is certainly the key I lost. Permit me to pay you for your trouble."

"It was no trouble at all, sir, and you don't owe me a cent," was the respectful but emphatic reply. "I found the key by the merest chance, and, noticing your advertisement this morning, brought it over at once, because I had nothing else to do. I am glad to have obliged you, but it really isn't worth talking about."

The banker smiled. "You are an American, aren't you?" he pleasantly asked.

"Yes, sir; from Chicago."

"A great city and a great country," he observed. "If you won't let me pay you for the key, at least tell me if there is anything I can do for you while you are in Sydney."

One of his happy inspirations seized Paul. "If you would be kind enough to give me a letter to the agents of the Orient Steamship Company I would be greatly obliged," he said. "I don't mind telling you that I have been trying for some time to get employment on one of their homeward-bound boats, but I don't receive any encouragement. A good word to the agents would be a great help, I am sure."

"I'll give you the letter with pleasure. I happen to know the gentlemen intimately. Let me have your name, please."

"Paul Travers, sir."

"Just be seated a few minutes, Mr. Travers, and you shall have what you want." Then he rang a bell and a stenographer appeared, to whom the banker dictated a short letter, overhearing which Paul mentally decided his vexations and disappointments were nearing an end.

"I gather you are trying to see a bit of the great world," remarked the bank manager while the letter was being typewritten.

"Yes, sir; for that reason I prefer the roundabout way home instead of returning to San Francisco. Not having much money, I, of course, work my passage from point to point. So far I have done fairly well, and with good luck I expect to be back in Chicago six months from now."

"And then what? A second long tramp in some other direction?"

"No, sir; I am planning to be a newspaper man and hope to go to work on one of the big Chicago dailies when I get back."

The door opened and a clerk brought in the expected letter. Taking the envelope, the banker wrote in the lower left-hand corner, "Introducing my young friend, Paul Travers." "There," he exclaimed, handing it over to Paul, "if that doesn't do the business, come back and let me know." Then he shook hands with the youngster as if he were really interested in him and wished him a safe and pleasant voyage back to America.

In the outer room Paul brushed by the pin-headed youth on the stool. "Good-bye, collars," he murmured as he passed. "Try to be a little more accommodating to the next stranger who wants to see your manager." Without waiting for a response or even turning his head to note the effect of this flippancy he kept serenely on through the office until he reached the street.

It was the junior member of the firm of steamship agents who received the letter of introduction which Paul brought from the banker. He told the lad it was beyond his power to make a position for him on any of the company's boats, but he would furnish him a letter of recommendation to the captain of the incoming steamer, which was due in a few days, and if there chanced to be a vacancy he had no doubt it would help him to secure it. Thankful enough to get this concession Paul went away, after arranging to call for the letter as soon as the Chimborazo was bulletined.

The four days intervening dragged heavily for the boy. With a voracious appetite and an almost empty purse, the problem of adjusting himself to these conditions was a trying one. By nice figuring, his finances would procure just five meals, so he was obliged to restrict himself to one a day. This he planned to eat at three o'clock in the afternoon, combining in it breakfast, dinner and supper. He avoided all exercise which had a tendency to increase the appetite, and to shorten the time between meals as much as possible he read assiduously in the public library. He usually visited the reading-room immediately after taking his combination meal, remaining there until the doors were closed at ten o'clock. Then he borrowed an interesting book from an attendant, went to his room and read till almost daybreak.

An economical sleep followed, lasting until two o'clock in the afternoon, by which time he was hungry clear through and nearly ready to dine off tenpenny nails. He found a restaurant where bread was placed on the table in generous quantities, and by filling up freely on this staple a shilling bought all he could eat in the way of meat and vegetables. Once in a while he managed to slip a double slice of bread and butter in his pocket for a midnight luncheon, but this was always a red-letter occasion.

The Chimborazo had scarcely made fast to her dock when Paul sought the captain and presented his credentials. Glancing over the letter, the skipper scribbled a few words across its face, and instructed the lad to present it to the chief steward. The latter was a keen-faced Englishman, with eyes that looked out from the corners, and a square, firm chin that denoted a constant exercise of authority. He read the letter very deliberately, meantime taking mental note of Paul's personal appearance.

"Ever do any stewarding?" he suddenly asked.

"Yes, sir."

"Got your sea legs, I suppose?"

"Yes, sir."

"When can you come to work?"

"In an hour."

"All right; get back here promptly and report to me."

This was the extent of his catechism, and that was the way in which Paul became one of the crew of the steamship Chimborazo, as stanch a vessel as ever breasted the waves of the Indian ocean or plowed between the sun-baked shores of the Suez canal.

On the ship's books he was rated merely as "general servant," in which classification all the understewards were entered. If Paul had an easy time ashore, he soon made up for it by his labors aboard the Chimborazo, which in the week prior to sailing he found arduous enough. He was one of a score of youngsters, ranging in age from sixteen to twenty, whose duties were confined exclusively to caring for the main deck and saloon when not engaged in waiting on passengers. The chief steward and his brawny first assistant saw to it that no one loafed or shirked his work, their constant supervision rendering any "soldiering" out of the question.

While the ship lay at her docks, and before the passengers came aboard, the lads were kept very busy scrubbing the paintwork, cleaning the silverware, getting in stores, and holystoning the main or saloon deck, which the sailors were not supposed to touch. Holystoning began immediately after coaling, which latter operation left the boards in inky blackness. It was a job the boys had to do on their hands and knees, pumice-stone instead of soap being the chief accessory in removing the dirt. Paul's back ached for a week following this assignment, while his skinned knees and sore fingers bore tribute to the thoroughness of his work.

But, after all, this task was not to be compared with his ice-packing experience, a chilly operation which sent the boy to his bunk with cholera cramps that threatened for a whole day to develop into a serious illness.

As the Chimborazo was bound for London via the Indian ocean, Red sea, Suez canal, and the Mediterranean, which meant five or six weeks of voyaging in the hottest latitudes, a goodly supply of ice was a very essential part of the commissariat, and to keep well it required close packing. Paul, with three others, was detailed to enter the freezing room and store the ice, neatly and compactly, as the huge blocks were sent below by means of a rope and tackle.

The compartment was long and narrow and the ceiling so low that as the tiers of ice uprose the boys were compelled to lie outstretched on the chilly blocks, in which awkward position they slid the big squares into place. Armed with a pick and with only a potato sack between his thin serge trousers and the icy surface, for nearly four hours Paul filled in the crevices with broken pieces, which had to be vigorously pounded home in order to make the ice pack thoroughly. In spite of the chilly atmosphere the lads perspired freely, and when their task was completed all four were in a state of physical exhaustion that threatened deleterious results. A double dose of brandy ordered by the doctor and a recommendation to strip and crawl between woolen blankets had a salutary effect, but for the succeeding twenty-four hours Paul lay groaning in his bunk with a severe and decidedly unromantic attack of cramps in his stomach. He was feeling better, but still unable to leave his berth, when the Chimborazo steamed out from her docks and headed for the Pacific ocean.

CHAPTER XVIII.

LIFE IN THE "GLORY HOLE."

THE sleeping apartment of the understewards was known as the "glory hole." Who first gave it this singular but striking title no one could tell, but the "glory hole" it had been far back in the earliest recollection of the oldest hand on shipboard.

It was appropriately named in many respects. Situated just forward of the main saloon, on the deck below, it was separated by a thin partition only from the hold, where the passengers' baggage was stored. A dark and dismal compartment at best, fitted up with a number of wooden bunks or "pews" and lighted by an oil lamp which swung from the center of the room, it illy accommodated the score of understewards, pantrymen and galley slaves who made life a burden to the head saloon steward.

The wit of the glory hole was a

genuine London cockney, nicknamed "Scully," from the fact that he filled the position of scullery boy in the cook's kitchen, where he furbished the pots, pans and copper kettles sacred to that department. He could neither read nor write, but was chock full of native humor, and his bright sallies kept his companions in a constant roar whenever he was below. It was he who christened Paul "Yank," and who established the newcomer in his strange surroundings by giving him the right hand of fellowship and welcoming him to the glory hole.

The name stuck to Paul throughout the voyage, and so long as he remained on shipboard no one ever thought of calling him anything else. Even the chief steward addressed him by this title, and on one occasion the pompous captain, making his morning round of inspection, inquired why "Yank's" blankets were not neatly folded and in their customary place at the head of his bunk.

Shipped at London and serving English owners, it naturally followed that all Paul's messmates were Britishers.

Many of them, like the witty but illiterate "Scully," were cockney born and bred, and their sublime disregard of the English language, particularly of the letter "h," was an unsolved puzzle over which Paul constantly marveled. Full of Whitechapel slang and concert hall ditties, there was yet nothing vicious about the youngsters, whose treatment of the American recruit was friendly enough, with one or two notable exceptions.

There were two pert cockney youths who did not take kindly to Paul's advent among them. From the outset they sneered at the "blawsted Yankee," whom they looked upon as an interloper and with whom they were constantly finding fault, to the great disgust of Paul's self-constituted friend, "Scully."

"W'y cawn't yer leave Yank alone?" he bawled from his pew the morning after sailing, when Paul, aching in every limb from his ice-packing experience, lay groaning in his bunk. "'E ain't a 'urtin' you blokes, is 'e?"

They had been making covert allusions to the lad's illness, intimating in a mean sort of way that he was too fond of his bunk and that his ailment was only a pretense. Too sick to make a vigorous protest, Paul could only feebly resent their insinuations, but he mentally vowed to have it out with them whenever he was well enough to stand up and take his medicine.

"Let 'em alone, Scully," he murmured to his friend, who occupied the adjoining pew. "I'll settle with 'em both just as soon as I'm able to get up; see if I don't."

"D'ye 'ear that, Bricksey? D'ye 'ear that, Jonas?" exclaimed Scully, scenting a battle royal from afar, and secretly exulting in the anticipated sport. "'E'll give you blokes a precious wiggin', 'e says, one o' these days."

Bricksey and Jonas were in the act of completing their toilets preparatory to waiting on the saloon table for breakfast. "W'enever 'e's ready," said lofty Mr. Jonas, buttoning on a celluloid collar, "I shall be most 'appy to meet 'im." "And as for me," chimed in Bricksey, "I'll punch 'is bloomin' 'ead with the greatest pleasure and without charge h'any time 'e wants the job done." At which flippancy both laughed uproariously, and sprang up the companionway to the deck above.

"Two nice cups o' tea, them ducks is, now ain't they?" observed Scully, sarcastically. "S'elp me bob, I'll lick 'em meself, Yank, if you don't, just to teach 'em good manners; they's too jolly flip, they is, for this 'ere glory 'ole."

At Melbourne Paul was able to crawl out of his bunk and renew his duties; a little shaky on his pins and still full of aches and pains, but too anxious to refute the insinuation that he was "soldiering" to occupy his pew any longer. More passengers and stores were taken aboard and then the Chimborazo steamed away to South Australia, where she was to make her last call in colonial waters. Anchoring in the beautiful semaphore of Port Adelaide, a quantity of flour and a dozen live steers were brought aboard in lighters, while a small tug conveyed the half dozen passengers booked from this port. Paul longed to go ashore to pay a farewell visit to his cousins, but the ship's stay was limited to a few hours, which effectually precluded a leave of absence.

From Adelaide the steamer headed direct for Cape Leewin, which is at the southern extremity of Western Australia and the last bit of land to be seen until Cape Guardafui, on the eastern coast of Africa, is sighted. In rounding this point vessels are pretty sure to encounter a heavy blow, Cape Leewin being a sort of miniature Cape Horn, with a gale of wind in constant readiness to let loose on the wary navigator.

The Chimborazo had to take her medicine with the rest, with, perhaps, a little extra dose of dirty weather by way of an Australian farewell. The wind blew almost a hurricane and the waves that dashed over the ship were so cold and came with such force that several of the steers on deck died from the exposure while dozens of chickens were drowned in their coops.

Paul witnessed an amusing incident during this blow. The gale was at its height when he relieved the "saloon watch" about midnight, and his instructions were to see that all the portholes were kept snug, as the Chimborazo was shipping considerable sea. The passengers had been warned before retiring to refrain from touching them, no matter how close the atmosphere became, but an obstinate John Bull thought he knew more than the officers and turned in, leaving the porthole in his berth partially open.

He was rudely awakened from sleep by a sudden rush of water through the orifice, which completely drenched the cabin and, pouring into his berth, half drowned the occupant. Scared nearly out of his wits, and almost choked with salt water, he leaped to the floor and darted into the saloon shrieking: "We're drowning, we're drowning!"

Guessing the cause of his fright, Paul ran by the excited Englishman and jumped for the open port in the stateroom. Taking advantage of a favorable lurch of the vessel, he slammed the iron frame shut and turned the screw before the next wave had a chance to force its way through. Meantime the rest of the passengers, catching the alarm, came rushing from their cabins, regardless of their costumes. Men in pajamas and women with faces as white as their nightrobes pounced upon Paul as he emerged from the flooded stateroom, all eager to learn the dire tidings. Quieting their fears by assuring them there was no danger, the lad hastily explained the cause of the commotion.

Then the women awoke to a sense of the proprieties, and, gathering their flowing garments about them, fled back to the privacy of their cabins. One stout colonial lady, who was in a particularly airy garb, grabbed the red piano cover to hide her exposed limbs, and whisked through the saloon like a flaming meteor, her flight hastened by an uncontrollable burst of laughter from two irreverent youngsters in pajamas who were not too scared to enjoy the ludicrous spectacle she presented.

Paul had a hard task mopping up the water in the Englishman's cabin. But there was some satisfaction in knowing that every stitch of clothing in it was soaked with salt water and completely spoiled. It was daylight before the lad restored order, and he felt he had fairly earned the piece of gold which the passenger insisted was due him for his trouble.

After this experience the Englishman never fooled with portholes, and on the hottest nights, while in the Red Sea, he lay half suffocated in his berth rather than take any chances with open ports.

After leaving Cape Leewin the weather moderated materially, but the first Sunday at sea it was still too rough to hold services on deck, so the passengers gathered in the main saloon, the captain officiating and the entire crew participating. As Paul was very tired, he passed the hour in his pew in rest and appropriate meditation, listening half dreamily to the running fire of cockney small talk indulged in by his comrades of the glory hole. So far he had avoided any direct quarrel with either Jonas or Bricksey, but every day their attitude toward him became more exasperating and unbearable, and the lad was nerving himself for the supreme moment when he felt sure he would be compelled to assert his manhood.

In the assignment of work among the understewards, to Paul had been given the task of waiting on the children's table. There were about a dozen little ones in the saloon, and they, together with several nurses who ate with them, were the lad's particular charges. It really meant so much extra work for him, as, their meals occurring half an hour in advance of the saloon table, he was expected to get everything cleared away before the regular meal times, in which he also had to lend a hand. There was no idling on board the Chimborazo, and those who have followed Paul's adventures thus far may judge for themselves whether the lad earned his salt these days. A glance at a sample day's work will better inform them how his time was occupied.

At 4:45 A. M. the "deck man" clattered down the companionway into the glory hole and aroused the tired occupants of the pews with a "Now, then, tumble out, fellows; two bells just gone. Pile up on deck lively!"

With many a yawn and muttered remonstrance the boys lazily dress and seek the purer air above. Each one is supplied with a bucket and scrubbing brush at the beginning of the voyage, for which he is held responsible. Any loss is charged to his account and deducted from his wages when the crew is paid off. Sometimes a boy loses his brush and bucket through carelessness, and these he tries to replace by poaching on his comrades' supplies, carefully erasing their private marks and substituting his own instead.

Paul's initial duty after turning out was to produce his bucket and brush from the dark corner under his pew, where they were secreted, and scrub fifty feet of the main deck, the allotment being made by the first assistant steward. This task generally consumed an hour and a half, and the boy found it a rather severe eye-opener. Following that came an hour's grind in the saloon, polishing the glasses in the racks or cleaning the brasswork on the punkah rods. At 7:30 he went below to dress for the children's breakfast at eight. At nine the regular saloon breakfast was served, after which he had thirty minutes to discuss his own meal, by this time an absolute necessity. His next move was to dive below into the glory hole to get his pew in readiness for morning inspection, and then came more cleaning in the saloon to prepare for the eagle eye of the captain on his grand rounds at eleven o'clock. Polishing skylights or silverware lasted until twelve o'clock, when the children's dinner had to be served. Saloon luncheon at one o'clock followed, after which, if it was not a "field day," the lads were allowed a short rest.

Twice a week, however, this much-needed respite was denied, what was known as "field days" occurring, when the afternoons were devoted to hauling flour, "spuds" and other supplies from the storeroom forward or passing up beer-cases from the lazarette, all of which were backaching jobs. At five o'clock, in the midst of a delightful nap, the harsh voice of the Scotchman, who ranked as head saloon steward, would penetrate the glory hole, and Paul would be awakened by the cry of "Oonder, below, Yank! Air ye comin' oop the noo?" And out "Yank" would have to tumble in order to serve the children's tea.

Saloon dinner at six was the event of the day, a two hours' task that was not completed until every bit of silver, glassware and crockery had been "strapped up" and stowed away in the pantryman's closet. Their own dinner the boys ate as they could find time after the last passenger had cleared out and before the work of "strapping up" began. Right on top of this came saloon tea at 8:30, a light meal, in which tea and toast predominated. Twice a week Paul's rest was broken by a midnight watch from twelve to two or from two to four, which duty, however, did not excuse him from the regular call at 4:45 in the morning. The boy did not put on much flesh during the seven weeks he served aboard the Chimborazo on that voyage from Sydney to London.

The second Sunday at sea was

marked by a burial, the first Paul had ever seen in the ocean, unless that of the performing stallion be considered. The day previous a young woman in the steerage had died of consumption. Her brother was taking her back to their native Wales to die, knowing she was beyond recovery. The young man was greatly affected during the impressive funeral services, and when the body, sewed up in canvas and weighted with iron slugs, was shot over the wooden grating his sobs were quite distressing. The funeral was held immediately after breakfast, all the passengers, fore and aft, gathering with uncovered heads about the captain, who read from the ritual the beautiful words appointed for burials at sea.

On the Wednesday following another death occurred, this time in the saloon. It happened during Paul's midnight watch. He had just returned from making the "grand rounds" in the second cabin and was trimming the oil lamp which swung from the rack, when he heard a faint cry in one of the staterooms. Knowing the doctor had been attending a sick passenger, the lad rightly guessed whence the sound issued and went direct to the invalid's cabin. The poor fellow was fighting for breath and was feebly beating the bedclothes when Paul opened the door. He summoned the doctor at once, but before the latter reached the sick man's room his services were not needed. The deceased had made a fortune in tin mining in New South Wales, but at the sacrifice of his health, his system having been ruined by lead-poisoning. At eight bells Thursday morning his emaciated body was consigned to the deep and all his effects placed in charge of the purser to be turned over to the relatives in England.

One morning, shortly before the ship crossed the equator, Paul reached under his pew for his bucket and found it gone. He was positive he had placed it there the day before, so he thought there was little doubt one of the boys had purloined it. But which one? With unerring intuition he decided that the thief was his arch-enemy, Jonas, whose own bucket, he happened to know, had been in a dilapidated condition for some time. Both Jonas and Bricksey had been particularly odious in their actions for several days, apparently with the intention of making life on the Chimborazo as uncomfortable as possible for the "Yankee interloper."

"W'at's wrong, Yank?" demanded Scully, noticing Paul's distress. "'As somebody been an' gone an' swiped yer paile?"

"Yes, bucket and brush have both disappeared."

"'Oo took 'em d'ye suppose?"

"Well, I don't know, for sure, but I think Jonas had a hand in it."

Jonas was just getting ready to climb the companion ladder, when the lad's challenging tones reached him.

He dropped back into the glory hole and stalked across the dimly lighted room to where Paul stood.

"You're a lyin' Yankee sneak!" he shouted, shaking his fist in the boy's face, "and for a thrupp'ny bit I'd lick the whole 'ide hoffer yer!"

The crucial moment had come. Paul caught a glimpse of Scully's tense expression and he felt that all the boys were watching him closely to see if he displayed the white feather. He knew he must either give this Whitechapel bully a good thrashing or else submit to continual indignities the remainder of the voyage.

The ugly face of Jonas was peering into his own and the little pig eyes wore so aggravating an expression that in an instant prudence had vanished and, shooting out his right hand, Paul dealt his adversary a ringing slap on the cheek.

Roaring like a bull, Jonas dashed for Paul's throat, but the youngster was too quick for him, and, leaping aside, again administered a smart clip, this time with his clenched fist.

"A ring, a ring!" yelled the boys, whose inherent British desire to see fair play was in the ascendant. "Keep'em apart, Scully, till we make a circle."

Scully had already darted in between the two angry lads. Inwardly realizing it would be a mistaken kindness toward Paul to prevent the fight, he hurriedly whispered to keep cool and "smash 'im 'atween the heyes hevery time."

Bricksey performed the friendly offices for his chum. The contestants, stripped to their waists, faced each other, and waited for Scully to call "time." Paul was pale, but determined, Jonas savage and flushed, the fingermarks on his cheek showing plainly even in that uncertain light.

"Don't let 'im close in on ye," was Scully's parting warning; "'e's strong as a 'orse on the crush."

The lad nodded and the two sparred for position. With his long arms Jonas had the advantage, but Paul was much more active, and the boys were by to see that no unfair advantage was taken.

A terrific left-hander aimed by Jonas was neatly guarded, and in retaliation the youngster got in a swinging overhand that landed under his opponent's right ear. Back and forth the blows passed in rapid succession, and when Scully called time both lads were pretty well winded. Paul's nose bled profusely from a tap early in the contest, but his adversary's left eye was almost closed and a front tooth was missing.

A brief rest and they went at it again, the one savagely determined to force the fighting, the other keenly alert to keep out of chancery and get

in as many telling whacks whenever the opportunities presented. In three minutes they had given and taken several vicious blows, and the punishment was beginning to tell. The perspiration poured down Paul's face and body in streams, so that he was almost blinded, while an ugly gash on his cheek added to his distress. But he had the grim satisfaction of knowing that Jonas was in even a worse condition, and he gritted his teeth for the third round.

Just as they engaged again and Paul had stopped a sudden rush by a well-aimed body blow the boys were electrified by hearing a well-known voice exclaim: "You young wretches, what do you mean by this sort of deviltry? Stop it this instant!"

In a second the ring had melted, and seizing their buckets the lads crowded up the ladder and disappeared. Jonas, too, had suddenly vanished, leaving Paul and Scully to confront the angry chief steward.

CHAPTER XIX.

ABOARD THE CHIMBORAZO.

Paul presented anything but an attractive appearance. Blood was streaming from the gash on his cheek, his lips were puffed out to two or three times their normal size, his left eye was partially closed, and a number of black and blue spots on his body were in painful evidence. The poor lad staggered back as the chief steward confronted him, and would have fallen but for Scully's assistance.

"What infernal nonsense have you been up to, Yank?" demanded his superior.

"'Tain't 'is fault, Mr. Masters," interposed Scully. "'E were driven to it, s'elp me! There's the chap as is to blame for this 'ere rumpus," and he pointed toward Jonas' pew.

The steward strode over to the bunk indicated and, reaching inside, grabbed the skulking occupant by an arm. "Come out o' that," he shouted "and show yourself; I'll teach you young savages to fight."

Groaning and mumbling, Jonas dragged his half-naked body to the center of the room. He wasn't a pretty sight, either. One eye was completely closed and the other was making sympathetic strides toward a like condition. His chest showed marks of severe punishment, and when he opened his lips to speak a yawning cavity denoted the absence of two front teeth.

"Now, what have you two fellows to say for yourselves that I shouldn't report you to the captain?" exclaimed the steward, critically surveying the sorry-looking couple, and striving hard to control his features. "He ought to masthead you both for twenty-four hours and put you on hardtack and water. Pretty looking objects you are, I must say."

"'E called me a liar," whined Jonas, "an' then 'e 'it me."

"He stole my bucket and brush, Mr. Masters," declared Paul, "and besides he has been annoying and insulting me ever since I came aboard. I couldn't stand it any longer and just had to fight him."

Perhaps the chief steward had some inkling of the true situation, or, it may be, considered the boys had received punishment enough, for he was a wise man of much experience in handling youngsters. Without revealing his thoughts, however, he sharply questioned Jonas.

"Did you take Yank's bucket? I want the truth, sir!"

"Ye-es," came the unwilling and surly response.

"Where is it?"

"Under my pew."

"Trot it out, quick!"

The thoroughly whipped bully fumbled under his bunk and presently produced the missing articles, with the initials "P. T." in plain view, as Paul quietly pointed out to the chief.

"Now, then, Jonas," demanded the steward, "what were you doing with Yank's property?"

"Nothink, upon me sivvey, sir; I took 'em just to make 'im wild, and was goin' to put 'em back harfter a bit."

The chief eyed him sharply, and although he may have thought the fellow was lying, he hadn't the heart to punish him further, for Jonas presented a most pitiable exterior. But discipline must be maintained, and his voice assumed its severest expression as he continued: "Very well, sir, I'll take your word for it, but mark me, boy, if I hear of any further trouble I'll lock you up in the lazarette long enough to induce a bitter repentance." Then turning to Paul he added: "I want no more fighting aboard this ship; if you can't get along without that just report to me, and I'll find out the reason why. Scully, I shall hold you responsible for the actions of Jonas and Yank, and shall expect you to keep order down here. Do you understand?"

"Yes, sir."

"All right, then get to work lively. As for you, Jonas, don't show that face of yours in the saloon until those eyes look half-way respectable. Yank, wash off that blood and go to work, and don't let me catch you disabling any more of my help or it may go hard with you." Then turning hastily to conceal a smile, the firm but really good-hearted steward sought the deck above.

And peace reigned again in the glory hole. Evidently Bricksey had no desire to run foul of the "American privateer," as some of the boys dubbed Paul after his battle, for he maintained a respectful distance, and took good care to keep his mouth shut. As for Jonas, he was as mum as an oyster; no amount of chaffing could elicit the slightest response from his closed lips. He had learned his lesson, and was disposed to profit by it, in all of which Paul secretly exulted, for he was naturally a peaceable lad, and had no desire to get into further embroilments with his shipmates.

So a truce was declared and the wounds gradually closed, but the great fight was a fruitful topic of conversation in the glory hole for weeks after. To this day the old-timers tell the newly joined cockney of the pitched battle they once witnessed at 5 o'clock in the morning between a big chap named Jonas and a plucky young American called "Yank," and when they are asked which whipped they shrug their shoulders and say, "Well, Yank went to work that same morning, but Jonas didn't show up on deck for three days."

The third day of July was the third Sunday at sea, and as the Chimborazo drew nearer the line the sun beat down with intense fervor. But a good breeze blew which made living just endurable, and as the passengers stood bareheaded on the upper deck listening to the service read by the captain Paul thought he had never seen a more attractive picture. The ocean was like glass, the quarter deck as spotless as successive holy-stonings could make it, and the sailors, in their bright blue jerseys, grouped among the passengers, lent just the requisite amount of color to the scene. The canvas, flapping lazily overhead, Paul likened to white wings of peace outstretched above the worshipers as if invoking a benediction.

Fourth of July the Chimborazo

crossed the equator. For days previous Paul had inwardly determined to celebrate, and, although he was the only American on board, he felt that he must not let the day pass without some attempt at glorification. Accordingly he invested nearly all his tips in lemonade, mild bottled beer, pipes, tobacco and cigars, intending to give a feast to his comrades. From the kitchen he begged a quantity of sandwiches, and the pastry cook agreed to smuggle down a lot of goodies from his cupboard. There were no formal invitations extended. From the "copy" furnished by Paul the purser's clerk engrossed a handsome page of foolscap in red and blue ink on white paper, bearing the general invitation, which the lad tacked up on the centerpost in the glory hole. Its composition afforded the boys considerable amusement. Even the lofty captain deigned to smile when at inspection the chief steward called his attention to the odd announcement. The notice was couched something like this:

> **AT SEA.**
> *July 4, 188—*
> ORIENT S. S. CHIMBORAZO.
>
> ---
>
> THE AMERICAN EAGLE WILL SCREAM IN THE GLORY HOLE THIS EVENING AT TWO BELLS, UNDER THE PERSONAL DIRECTION OF "YANK" TRAVERS.
>
> ---
>
> ALL OCCUPANTS OF PEWS ARE CORDIALLY INVITED TO HEAR THE GREAT BIRD OF FREEDOM SHRIEK AND TO INSPECT HER TAIL FEATHERS.
>
> ---
>
> THERE WILL BE GOOD THINGS TO EAT, GOOD THINGS TO DRINK, GOOD TOBACCO TO SMOKE AND A HIGH OLD TIME GENERALLY.
>
> ---
>
> P. S.—Guests are kindly requested to refrain from plucking the bird's plumage. Come early and avoid the rush.

The entertainment was a huge success. Paul was quite a favorite with the boys, and they attended his jollification en masse, heedless of the fact that they were asked to celebrate the defeat of the British flag and the birthday of the republic wrested from the hands of their own monarchical forefathers. Paul's speech, too, was enthusiastically received. It was beautifully short and to the point. When Scully pounded on the center post for order and asked permission to "interduce" his "pertickler friend, Yank," there was a yell of approval, in the last throes of which the orator of the day jumped on the table and, straddling a plate of beans, waved a hand for attention.

"Fellow-messmates:" he began. "In my country Fourth of July is a famous holiday; everybody takes a day off then to hear the national bird scream and to see her spread her tail feathers. The eagle, as some of you may know, is our emblem of freedom and is held in much the same regard as the British lion is by all true Englishmen. This is the anniversary of the day when the American eagle twisted the British lion's tail until he roared with pain and let go his grip of the American colonies forever. The eagle and the lion have been good friends ever since, bar one or two little spats that have long since been forgiven and forgotten. The real American is so closely allied to the Englishman that it wouldn't surprise me at all if I could trace relationship to half you fellows in the glory hole. But life is short, and there are things more pressing before us. As an American I am glad to welcome you to this humble feast, and as good Englishmen I shall expect you to sweep the board. I will now propose the health of the American eagle—long may she scream. (Ah! thank you, gentlemen, that was very handsome.) And now, please, a bumper in honor of the well-fed and eminently respectable British lion—long may he roar."

The cheers were given with a will, and as Paul leaped from his perch the lads gave a three-times-three for their host, after which they fell to on the lemonade, mild beer and eatables he had provided. Then the long "churchwardens" were brought out and the pipes of peace puffed until the smoke in the glory hole was thick enough to cut with a knife. But the big ventilator running from the deck above was brought into play, and when the fog lifted the boys called on Paul for a song.

"Come, Yank, pipe up," they insisted.

"Yes, cut loose, old fellow; give us 'Yankee Doodle.'"

"No, no," laughed Paul, "not that; I'll give you an air with which you are all familiar. Your countrymen swear we stole it from your 'God Save the Queen,' but my people declare you adopted it from an old Slav air, so I guess that evens it up."

Then in a clear voice, Paul began:

> "My country, 'tis of thee,
> Sweet land of liberty."

The boys listened intently to the end. An encore being demanded, with graceful tact he started "God Save the Queen," which brought all the loyal lads to their feet, and, joining in with a will, they fairly made the boards creak. Paul's Fourth of July celebration was voted a magnificent success.

Cape Guardafui was sighted next day—the first land raised in three weeks, after a run of nearly six thousand miles. The coast line is very bold and rugged, and is so dangerous that mariners give it a wide berth. In addition, the natives are noted for their treachery and inhospitality, few castaways ever escaping from their clutches.

Five days later the Chimborazo passed the port of Aden on the Arabian coast, the coaling station for the peninsular and orient steamships, but as the orient liners coal at Port Said, no stop was made. Next morning the big steamer entered the Red Sea through Bab-el-Mandeb, or "Gates of Hell."

"Sizzling" hot better describes the atmospheric condition on shipboard than any other term, and if Paul had previously wondered at the significance of the Arabic for "hell gates" he no longer questioned its appropriateness. Several wrecks were sighted on the way to Suez, the deserted hulks standing high and dry on the sand close to the African shore.

Naturally enough the lad was eager to get a first glimpse of the famous Suez canal, that marvelous triumph of engineering skill which so endeared the indomitable De Lesseps to the French people, whose confidence in him not even the disastrous Panama canal venture could entirely shake. The white stone government building adjoins the entrance to the great canal so closely that the architectural details could be seen from the deck of the Chimborazo. Vessels going through are restricted to a speed of five miles an hour, which makes a tedious passage, particularly as no travel is permitted after dark.

At the second station, where the Chimborazo was held over night, Paul and Scully took a plunge overboard, swimming from the African to the Arabian shore. But the current was so strong that when they landed on the sandy beach they found they had been carried fully three hundred yards below the vessel. In returning, they ran along shore until the boat lay a corresponding distance down stream, when they took to the water, and after an easy swim brought up alongside and were hauled aboard.

From one station to another the ship was attended by brown-skinned young Arabs, who ran along the sandy shores of the canal begging "backsheesh," to obtain which they plunged into the water whenever the pennies were flung from the quarter deck. Boys and girls, anywhere from ten to fourteen, followed the vessel on a dog-trot for hours, none of them wearing a scrap of clothing. Another feature that impressed Paul was the number of small, wooden crosses that lined the upper banks of the canal, marking the burial places of hundreds of laborers whose lives were forfeited during the process of construction. It is said that the building of the Suez canal cost the lives of over five thousand human beings.

A motley crowd of natives offering all kinds of barter awaited the steamer at Port Said, which was reached early on a Sunday morning. Almost as soon as the Chimborazo dropped her anchor she was surrounded by a frantic lot of boatmen who yelled their wares in execrable English and sold alleged curios to the passengers at ten times their actual value. Big lighters loaded with coal soon appeared, and a gang of scantily dressed fellahs, each provided with a "couffin," or willow basket, began trotting up the runway leading to the coal bunkers, into which the contents of their baskets were quickly dumped, the procession never stopping for three hours, when five hundred and sixty tons had been deposited in the steamer's hold by the indefatigable natives. Port Said and Singapore are considered the two fastest coaling stations in the world.

Leaving Port Said in the afternoon, Paul soon had his first sight of the Mediterranean Sea, through the blue waters of which the Chimborazo glided as if her nose already scented the white cliffs of England. The lights of Alexandria were discernible at dusk, but to the lad's great regret no call was made at this most ancient of Mediterranean ports. Past the Island of Crete, where Paul's sainted namesake is said to have been wrecked on his voyage to Rome, and on past the massive cone of Mt. Ætna, with its blue flames dancing upward, steamed the Chimborazo, until the Straits of Messina were entered, Stromboli left in the rear and the Bay of Naples reached at last.

After a magnificent night spent in the beautiful bay, with a pyrotechnic display from Vesuvius, that Paul knew was made extra fine for his sole benefit, the big liner lifted her anchor and bore away for Plymouth, her next port of call. The rock of Gibraltar held more of interest for the young traveler than any other spot in the Mediterranean, and he gladly arose an hour earlier than usual to gaze on this historic pile. A glass borrowed from the doctor the night previous enabled him to take a good look at the famous stronghold, about which clings so many old world romances. The signal station on the higher of the two peaks he could see quite plainly, and he fancied he caught a glimpse of a redcoat on sentry duty. Cape de St. Vincent was passed the next morning, and at seven in the evening the bo's'n, pointing to a few scattered lights in the distance, told Paul they marked the location of Lisbon.

About midnight the Chimborazo entered the Bay of Biscay, across which she had a good run to Plymouth, nothing of interest occurring beyond the death of a steerage passenger, who was buried abreast of the Island of Ushant, making the third death during the voyage. The new Eddystone lighthouse was passed just before dark, and at eight o'clock the anchor was dropped in Plymouth Bay. Here a few passengers went ashore, but the majority went on up the English channel to Gravesend, where a general exodus occurred.

Their departure was the signal for an unwonted activity among Paul's messmates, whose speculations for days previous had been based on the size of the tips they hoped to receive. This was a novel experience to Paul, but as he was there as a Roman among Romans he thankfully accepted the largesse that fell to his lot, a goodly portion of which came from the parents of the children whom he had attended so assiduously during the voyage.

Among the passengers whose acquaintance he had cultivated was the manager of the Beaver line of steamers, plying between Liverpool and Montreal. Shortly before Gravesend was reached the gentleman gave Paul his card and told the lad that when he was ready to cross the Atlantic he would help him to a berth on one of his boats. Naturally this kind offer was gratefully received, for the boy had not forgotten the vexatious delays and disappointments experienced at San Francisco, Dunedin and Sydney while trying to "get a ship."

The crew was paid off at the Royal Albert dock in London, where the lad received his wages account and certificate of discharge, with its accompanying "reward of merit" voucher. This evidenced that Paul Travers, shipped at Sydney as general servant and discharged at London, was accounted "very good in whatever capacity engaged," and with an established reputation for excellent conduct. These precious documents Paul carefully stowed away as souvenirs of his voyage, always to be preserved. He was back in the glory hole, in fact, placing the papers in his valise when Jonas dropped down the companionway.

"Look 'ere, Yank," said the latter, holding out his hand, "I s'pose you don't bear h'any malice, do you? I was a bit nawsty when you first came aboard, but I 'ope you've forgotten all that, hold chap, 'aven't you?"

"Oh, yes, long ago," returned Paul heartily, giving the proffered hand a good shake. "When we fought it out and quit I buried the hatchet, and I think you did the same. If you ever get to Chicago look me up, Jonas, and I shall be very glad to show you around. Good-bye, old fellow, remember me to Bricksey."

As Paul stepped out on the wharf with his satchel in his hand he halted to take a farewell look at the stout vessel, now given over to the noisy steam winches and shouting dock laborers engaged in unloading her cargo.

"She's a darlin', my boy, ain't she?" sung out a well-known voice, and the next minute Scully had seized his bag and was hurrying him across the dock to a cab he had in waiting.

"Myke 'aste, Yank," he urged; "honly got 'arf a jiffy to get to the Pig and W'istle, w'ere the rest of the blokes is. Just a little good-bye sort of a blow-hout, you know," he explained, "and we want you to jine us. Jump hin, old chap!"

Laughing and half protesting, Paul suffered himself to be hustled into the cab, and heard Scully tell the driver to "clap on hall sail for the Pig," at which cozy inn Paul found eight or nine of his late comrades of the glory hole.

It was a very jolly dinner. Good English roast beef, with Yorkshire pudding and a deep-dished gooseberry pie that would have made even Carlyle grin, were the chief concomitants, with vegetables galore on the side and genuine old English ale, "right from the tap, ye know," as the waiter assured Paul. It was almost dark before the lad finally broke away from the happy youngsters, whose farewells wound up with the ringing chorus

> For he's a jolly good fellow,

which his friend Scully had started.

CHAPTER XX.

HEADED FOR HOME.

Paul's desire to get away from the "Pig and Whistle" was due solely to his anxiety to obtain the letters which he knew must be awaiting him at the American Exchange in the Strand, to which address he had directed his people to write. It was after nine o'clock when he registered at "Gillig's," and on payment of a small sum was accorded the privileges of the exchange for one month. But better than his card of admission was the budget of letters which the clerk handed out all bearing the Chicago postmark. There was one among them that caused his heart to flutter wildly, and perhaps all his boy friends will sympathize with the over-powering curiosity which tempted him to tear that open before reading the home news.

On the envelope, in bold black type,

was printed "The Chicago Mercury," and the easy-running superscription was so clearly professional that Paul knew instinctively it was from Mr. Wilder. He was not mistaken. The managing editor of the Mercury wrote as follows:

DEAR PAUL—Your two breezy letters were received in due season, and were promptly printed in the Mercury. I want to compliment you on the excellent story of the shipwreck, and to say that it has been favorably mentioned by a number of competent critics. Your visit to Fiji was also well told and proved an interesting feature of the Sunday paper. I am convinced you have not mistaken your field, and if you do not get drowned crossing the Atlantic, that position on the Mercury staff will be ready for you on your return to Chicago. Feeling certain you will need a little cash when you get to London, I am inclosing you a draft for £10 in payment of the two articles already published. We have one more on hand, which we shall use next Sunday, and if you send me your New York address, I will remit to that point. Your people are all well, but very anxious to see you safe home again. With warmest regards and congratulating you on your plucky journey, I am, sincerely your friend,

FRANC B. WILDER.

Paul's cheeks flushed with gratified pleasure. Praise from Sir Hubert was praise indeed, and that the great editor meant what he said was evidenced by the handsome check he inclosed. Oh, it was too good, too delightful, to be true, and for five minutes the lad could do nothing but gaze at the piece of stamped paper he held in his hand. What a lot of presents he could buy for his father, mother and the girls! And how thoughtful of Mr. Wilder to forward the money to London instead of waiting until he reached Chicago. He must write an acknowledgment at once, thanking his kind friend.

But there were his other letters awaiting a reading, and as Paul glanced at the untouched envelopes he blushed to think how nearly he had forgotten them in the contemplation of Mr. Wilder's words of praise. For an hour he was oblivious of England, of London, of Gillig's, as he read the closely written pages that chronicled the fortunes of the Travers family on the other side of the Atlantic. And all were well, too, but, oh, so anxious to get their truant boy back after his long absence. "We read your story of the shipwreck in the Mercury," wrote Madge, "and could hardly believe they were your own experiences. Mother cried, but I told her I was sure it was only a yarn you were spinning just to get your hand in. Own up, now, that 90 per cent was fiction."

"That's it," grumbled Paul, when he came across this frank criticism. "The old story of the prophet that couldn't command respect in his own country. I suppose my friends will believe all the fairy tales I spring and think they are perfectly natural, while at the genuine adventures they'll point the finger of scorn and reject them as rank impositions."

When Paul awoke next morning in the clean little room of the lodging house to which he had been directed by the clerk at Gillig's, he suddenly realized that it was his eighteenth birthday—one year and three months since he started on his long tramp around the world. He decided that he ought to celebrate it in a way that would leave a lasting impress on his mind, and, after studying a guidebook at the exchange, concluded that a visit to Westminster Abbey, the Tower of London and the British Museum would make a fitting holiday.

To the new-world youngster that ramble through the aisles of the cathedral, sacred to the memory of so many great men with whose names and deeds Paul was more or less familiar, was full of inspiring thoughts. He gave a little start on finding himself facing the bust of Major André, whom the sturdy Americans had hanged as a spy, but whom the British revere as a hero and a martyr.

"Ah! it's the point of view, after all," he mused, when he had partially recovered from the shock. "Of course André was a hero in the eyes of his countrymen, just as Captain Paul Jones was a hero in the estimation of all good Americans, and yet the Britishers class Jones as a pirate of the bloodthirstiest kind. There are always two sides to every proposition."

When he came to the plain marble slab bearing the name of ·Charles

Dickens, he stood pensively before it and murmured: "Great master, rather would I have been the creator of Sydney Carton and Barnaby Rudge than be President of the United States. Your fame is secure as long as the English language is read or spoken."

The "beef-eaters" at the tower, costumed just as in the days of bluff King Hal, he studied with curious interest. He had read, somewhere, years before, that the term "beef-eater" was an English corruption of the French word, "buffetier," or attendant, so was not misled when a loquacious tourist attempted to explain that the name was given on account of the prodigious quantity of roast beef they used to consume in olden times. However, Paul thanked the Kansas City man very politely and did not try to undeceive him. He visited the room where Lady Jane Gray was immured and was also shown her name, "Jane," scratched on the wall of the chamber where her husband, the unfortunate Lord Dudley, was confined.

The damp dungeons below, where dangerous political prisoners were incarcerated, had quite a fascination for the lad, and as he passed through the river gate, by which route so many ill-starred statesmen were led to execution, a vision arose of the courtly figure of Sir Thomas More thanking the governor of the tower for the kind attentions bestowed during his period of imprisonment. The crown jewels were interesting only because of the thrilling story they recalled of Colonel Blood's daring attempt to carry them off, but to the old captured cannon lying outside the walls he gave critical attention and spent over an hour trying to decipher the curious lettering, principally in French and Spanish, that was engraved on some of the rusty pieces of ordnance.

The afternoon was so far gone before he finally left the tower that his visit to the British Museum had to be deferred until next day, when the lad fairly reveled in the antiquities there contained. It would be useless to attempt a recital of what most attracted him—those of Paul's admirers who are interested must register a vow to explore this wonderful storehouse for themselves some day—but his enthusiasm was so great that he had to be driven out by the attendants when the hour of closing arrived, and then for the first time in ten hours he discovered he was hungry.

The record of the succeeding fortnight is one of sightseeing entirely. All the famous nooks about which he had read or of which he had heard were visited, not forgetting the haunts of his favorite Dickens, and including an exploration of Petticoat Lane and the famous Seven Dials. These trips, of course, made some inroads on his purse, but the lad soon learned to travel inexpensively, and previous severe experiences had instilled a spirit of economy that was highly creditable. On his jaunts about London he managed to pick up a number of pretty souvenirs and presents to carry home, which he knew would be fully appreciated by the recipients, and these, together with his Australian curios, made a very respectable and interesting collection.

But it was a piteous appeal from his mother, written in reply to the letter sent on his arrival in London, that put a sudden end to his rambles. It gave the lad an acute attack of homesickness not to be resisted, so, forswearing all further explorations, he bought a ticket to Liverpool and left London that same day.

At 5 o'clock in the evening Paul walked into the manager's office of the Beaver Line Steamship Company and presented the card that had been given him aboard the Chimborazo.

"Ah, it's you, my lad, is it?" exclaimed the manager, coming forward. "Tired of London so soon?"

"Not tired exactly, but desperately homesick," returned Paul smilingly.

"And want to get a ship, I suppose, eh?"

"Yes, sir, if you please."

"Well, you're in luck. The Winnipeg was to have sailed at six o'clock, but she is delayed four hours on account of a slight break in her machinery. I will give you a note to her captain, and you can pull out and present it as soon as you please."

Paul sincerely thanked the manager for his interest, and in half an hour was on the Mersey with a Liverpool boatman, en route to the Winnipeg. The captain was a bluff old Canadian, who consigned Paul at once to the steward, with instructions to put him to work, and before the ship weighed her anchor the lad was cleaning silver in the pantry, having signed papers for Montreal.

Compared with the Chimborazo, Paul had a very easy time on the Winnipeg. There was no loafing, but with only thirty saloon passengers and very few in the steerage, the demands on his services were infinitely lighter, so that the trip across the Atlantic was almost like a pleasure trip.

The first week out the ship met strong head winds and experienced pretty rough and rolling weather, but on the second Sunday the day was perfect, and all the passengers turned out on deck to enjoy the beautiful prospect. The ocean was as calm and peaceful as an artificial lake. As the Winnipeg entered the Straits of Labrador she was obliged to run at half speed, owing to a very thick fog, but in a few hours it lifted and the boat went ahead again. This was the only fog encountered during the voyage.

Early Monday morning, just nine days out from Liverpool, Paul had his first view of the St. Lawrence River. At Father Point the pilot was taken aboard and at midnight the steamer anchored at Point Levi, Quebec. The day following was spent in discharging part of the cargo, but Wednesday morning the voyage was resumed and Thursday Montreal was reached. Here Paul received his certificate of discharge, together with a $10 bill for his services, which, with a few presents from the passengers, again placed him in funds and insured his passage to Chicago in case of a failure to receive Mr. Wilder's remittance at New York.

But the managing editor had not forgotten his promise, and at the New York office of the Mercury Paul found a brief note, and accompanying it was a draft for $25. A letter from his father inclosed a trip pass over the Erie lines to Chicago, the receipt of which greatly elated the youth, for it meant that he could make good his boast of getting back to Chicago with more money in his pocket than he had at the start.

With a view to surprising his family Paul purposely refrained from telegraphing his prospective arrival, so that not a soul was present to meet him when the train rolled in at the terminal station at Chicago. Eager to get home, the lad threw his valise into the first cab he saw and told the driver to make the best time he could to the corner of Hoyne avenue and Adams street, where he planned to alight and walk to the house unobserved.

It was just dusk when Paul stole up the back porch of the modest cottage in which he and his two sisters were born. A gas jet was burning in the kitchen, and through the screen window he could see Madge and Edith putting away the supper dishes. The screen door was unlatched, and, pushing it gently open, he suddenly dropped his valise on the kitchen floor.

Both girls turned quickly, and, not immediately recognizing their brother, gave a short scream, which was abruptly checked by a cry of "Oh, it's Paul, it's Paul!" and the next instant his sisters were folded to his heart.

Such a crying! Such a kissing! In the midst of which in came their mother to learn the cause of the hubbub.

Well, there are some scenes that are too sacred to be described, and that meeting of Paul and his mother was one of them. When the lad finally disengaged himself to receive the embraces of his father, who had stood in the doorway watching this joyous reunion, the tears were flowing fast down his face, and the poor boy could illy control his voice. That was a very happy hour for the Travers family, however.

"But why didn't you write, you naughty boy?" demanded Edith later when they all sat around in hero worship of the prodigal. "You had no business to surprise us this way. Think what a risk you ran."

"Oh, he's used to risks," broke in Madge, "besides which joy seldom kills, does it, mother?"

"I never heard of it doing so, dear, and, you know, 'all's well that ends well.'" She was stroking Paul's hair as she spoke, but a minute later she uttered a startled cry and exclaimed: "Dear me, here we have been talking two hours, and no one has thought to ask if Paul has had his supper. Why, how thoughtless of us!"

"Now, mother, don't worry, I'm not a bit hungry," insisted Paul; but his mother had already flown to the kitchen, followed closely by Madge and Edith.

It was long after midnight before they thought of retiring, and even then they went upstairs and lingered on the landing for half an hour longer, still plying Paul with questions.

In his own room at last the lad stood, and his first act was to drop on his knees beside the white iron bed in which he had slept since he was a boy of ten. An hour later, when his mother stole in to see if he was really there yet, the moonlight played across his face, and as she pressed a kiss on the closed eyes she murmured a fervent "Thank God" for giving her back her only son.

And now, having brought Paul home safe and sound from his long journey of 50,000 miles, all who have followed his adventurous career will be interested in learning how he was received at the Mercury office. Before he had been in Chicago twenty-four hours he went down town to pay his respects to Mr. Wilder. With a curious trepidation he knocked at the editor's door, and the next minute was back again in the well-remembered room.

It was not strange that the busy newspaper man failed to identify in the bronzed face of the sturdy youth the rather delicate features of the lad from whom he had parted sixteen months before. But when Paul smiled and held out his hand there came instant recognition.

"Why! Why! Why! Is it possible that the young globe-trotter has returned?" he exclaimed with a hearty emphasis. "Sit down, sit down, my son; you don't know how delighted I am to see you. When did you get back?"

"Last night, sir."

"Last night! Then you must have surprised the folks, for I saw your father yesterday morning, and he hadn't heard a word since you left London."

"Yes, I wanted to break in on them without any fuss, so I didn't telegraph from New York, but came right through."

"Do you know, I'm proud of your record, Paul," said the editor presently, after the lad had expressed his gratitude for past kindnesses; "and before I forget it I want to say that you have well earned the right to wear a Mercury star. When will you be ready to begin work?"

"Next Monday, if agreeable, Mr. Wilder. I want to visit this week with the folks, and then I shall be anxious to make a start. Will that suit your convenience?"

"Oh, yes, any time. Get rested up good, and then report to me. By the way, Paul, how about that money you were to have when you reached Chicago?"

"Thanks to you, sir, I was able to keep my word. As you know, I had a little over fifty dollars when I left home. Well, your last draft that was awaiting me in New York is still in my pocket, together with nearly forty dollars in cash, so you see I have made good my boast."

Mr. Wilder laughed long and heartily. "That beats any record I ever knew," he finally declared. "Left here with fifty dollars in your purse, been gone nearly a year and a half, traveled upward of fifty thousand miles, and turn up with something over sixty dollars. Why, of course we want you on the Mercury staff; you're a marvel, that's what you are. The Society of Economic Research ought to make you an honorary life member."

The editor was still chuckling when Paul went away with instructions to report for duty to the city editor the following Monday. As the lad retired Mr. Wilder exclaimed under his breath: "A dangerous experiment, as I allowed, but it is the making of him."

* * * * * *

The story of Paul's first adventures ends here. Of his experiences as a reporter and later of his newspaper and literary successes something may be told at a future date. But it may be said that when he first pinned on his reporter's star it was with an inward resolve to be true to his ideals; to allow no personal prejudices to bias his writings, and to strive always to tell the truth. In this he has remained steadfast, although not without many struggles and temptations to secede. In Mr. Wilder he retained a warm friend, who was always glad to give kindly advice to the youngster whom he had practically inducted into journalism and over whose welfare he closely watched.

With Dr. Tolman Paul maintained a faithful correspondence. The doctor threatens every year to visit America, but so far has never made good his promise, although he is still a bachelor. "Jim" sticks to Australia, and Grand Rapids is the loser by it, for, having turned his mechanical genius to practical inventions, he is now doing very well in Melbourne. Every little while Paul sees a face on the street that is strangely familiar, but so far none of the many friends he made on his eventful trip has come to claim his attention.

A year after his return home he read that Ethel's father had been transferred from Fiji to a more lucrative diplomatic post near home, and when Paul goes abroad again he thinks he will certainly renew their friendship. But the lad may lose all interest long before the opportunity arrives.

Someone suggested to him a few months after he went to work on the Mercury that an account of his tramp around the world would make an interesting story for all youngsters fond of adventure, and Paul promised to write it out as soon as he found time. But I don't suppose he ever will, do you?

THE END.

www.ingramcontent.com/pod-product-compliance
Lightning Source LLC
Chambersburg PA
CBHW032014220426
43664CB00006B/237